IRS Managing Confl
Workplace

Consultant Editor
Heather Falconer

Routledge
Taylor & Francis Group

LONDON AND NEW YORK

First published by LexisNexis

This edition published 2011 by Routledge
2 Park Square, Milton Park, Abingdon, Oxon OX14 4RN
711 Third Avenue, New York, NY 10017, USA

Routledge is an imprint of the Taylor & Francis Group, an informa business

© Taylor & Francis Ltd 2004

Crown copyright material is reproduced with the permission of the Controller of HMSO and the Queen's Printer for Scotland. Any European material in this work which has been reproduced from EUR-lex, the official European Communities legislation website, is European Communities copyright.

A CIP Catalogue record for this book is available from the British Library.

ISBN 0 7545 2392 6

Typeset by Columns Design Ltd, Reading, England.

Foreword

Recent years have seen upheaval in the workplace on an unprecedented scale. Changes in the legal framework, coupled with the shock of an economic downturn and simultaneous boost in spending on public services, have left many organisations struggling to keep up. Small wonder, then, that in dealing with the need to restructure, refocus and rethink what they are all about, many have also experienced an increase in workplace conflict.

To some extent, this is reflected in the rising number of days lost to industrial disputes (albeit that this tends to reflect small numbers of strikes against a few very large employers). But new rights to protection against discrimination on grounds of religious belief and sexual orientation (soon to be joined by age), the extension of working time and flexible working legislation, and the growth of a 'rights culture' generally have also produced potential flashpoints.

The task of dealing with all this, and finding a harmonious – or at least survivable – way of encouraging creative conflict while containing the harmful variety, falls both on human resource professionals and, as IRS research has consistently found, increasingly on line managers. In small and medium-sized companies in particular, this can be a heavy burden to carry.

New Regulations and a revised ACAS code of conflict on discipline and grievances planned for Autumn 2004 should help to some extent – though getting to grips with official expectations about dispute resolution procedures will inevitably prove to be a demanding task in itself. We hope, therefore, that in this book you will find the tools you need to survive and flourish in that difficult environment.

Our thanks, as ever, go to the vast number of employers who answer our endless questions about their workplace realities and help us to formulate some shared solutions.

Mark Crail
Managing Editor
IRS Employment Review

About the authors

Consultant Editor

Heather Falconer

Heather Falconer is a freelance journalist and editor with 13 years' experience of specialising in HR and employment law issues for both the trade and national press. She was editor of *Employers' Law* from 1999 to 2003.

heather.falconer@rbi.co.uk

Contributors

David Liddle

David Liddle has extensive experience of mediation and conflict resolution within a variety of contexts. In 1994, whilst based in Leicester, he established one of the first community mediation schemes in the UK. Subsequently, he went on to establish the Conflict Resolution in Schools Programme (CRISP), was a founding member of the Midlands Mediation Network and was active in national and international mediation, conflict resolution and community cohesion programmes.

In 1998, David established Total Conflict Management Ltd. Based in the Centre for Workplace Mediation, Total Conflict Management offer high quality and innovative responses to workplace conflicts and disputes. They provide mediation and conflict resolution services to public, private and voluntary organisations and have taken a leading role in developing national practice standards for workplace mediators including the development of the national certificate in workplace mediation skills.

David has established numerous in-house workplace mediation schemes, undertaken mediation interventions in a wide variety of workplace disputes and has undertaken extensive research into the effectiveness of mediation and alternative dispute resolution (ADR). In 2003 David was awarded his MBA with distinction having undertaken detailed research into the effectiveness of mediation within organisational grievance, bullying and harassment policies and procedures.

david.liddle@tcmsolutions.co.uk

Mike Bagshaw

Dr Mike Bagshaw is a psychologist with over 15 years of organisational consultancy experience in the UK and abroad. He has worked with a wide range of organisations in both the private and public sector, helping them to overcome people management and development issues.

He is also an experienced one-to-one coach, working with those people in organisations who represent the critical intellectual capital for the future.

Mike began his career as a prison psychologist, where he designed and delivered courses for prison officers, and developed programmes for rehabilitation, pre-release, and suicide prevention. In 1988, he changed direction, and joined the world of commerce.

He started as a consultant for CEPEC, where he developed new programmes for management training. Some of these dealt with the trauma of violent incidents, from minor assault to bank raids, as well as how to defuse situations, even in the heat of battle. Mike has designed conflict management programmes for situations as varied as the normal office wranglings to being threatened at gunpoint.

In 1994 he became Development Director of Coutts Consulting, a position he held until 1998 when he co-founded Trans4mation, a management consultancy for training in leadership, management development, managing diversity and conflict mediation.

mike.bagshaw@trans4mation.com

Diane Hall

Diane is a senior specialist who has worked for over 13 years in the NHS in various senior positions. She has a wide range of experience covering medical staffing, organisational re-structuring, employee relations, the development and implementation of an Equalities and Diversity strategy and the implementation of complex change programmes. She has recently completed a Masters degree at Birkbeck College, London University and her special research interest was workplace bullying and the analysis of discourse.

Diane's last permanent post in the NHS was as Head of Corporate HR Services at Barts and The London NHS Trust. She currently works as a freelance HR consultant and interim manager.

dihall@btinternet.com

Marion McCrindle

Marion McCrindle is freelance HR consultant with many years' experience as an HR director in both the private and the public sector. Longstanding experience of dealing with unions and internal conflict issues, and training in handling conflict on a personal and operational level informs her writing and her consultancy work.

Turning to HR after early positions in operational work, finance, legal services and international marketing, Marion also sustains interim positions, if possible, in the public sector where institutional conflict can appear most obvious. Her private caseload is predominantly concerned with cases of bullying and disciplinary issues.

A growing passion for geology, she says, keeps this day-to-day involvement with work conflict in elegant perspective.

marion.mccrindle@btconnect.com

Contents

Chapter One
Conflict in the Workplace

Heather Falconer and Mike Bagshaw

INTRODUCTION

Whether it was Sir Alex Ferguson's unfortunate dressing room rage or the foul-mouthed bully tactics of City broking bosses, 2003 seemed to be a bumper year for high-profile conflict in the workplace.

And it wasn't just premier football clubs and the high-octane financial sector that hit the news. Sexual harassment, racism, bullying and generally oppressive behaviour have all made unwelcome headlines for numerous employers and institutions in the recent past.

We could be forgiven for thinking that destructive conflict is gaining a disturbing foothold in UK workplaces. But is it so?

Workplace conflict has always been with us, and eradicating it all together would be disastrous. Indeed, as the examples above illustrate, many creative, high-performance workplaces appear to thrive on it. If there is only one point of view, there will be only one way forward, and it may not be the best way. It is better to explore many possibilities, and that can only happen if there are lots of ideas around. Whenever there is more than one idea, there will be conflict between views. But this conflict of opinion can be positive – it can provide impetus for change and be constructive. As long as the conflict is constructive not destructive, it can be a force for change and progress.

WHAT ARE THE BENEFITS OF CONSTRUCTIVE CONFLICT?

Awareness – People who learn to deal with disagreement come to recognise their personal conflict style, and the effect they have on others. They find out where their strengths and weaknesses are, and this equips them to deal better with future conflicts.

Better solutions – When people disagree about a plan of action, it gets them thinking. They often look again at the plan and notice defects. When nobody raises any doubts, the first plan just goes through.

Reduces 'groupthink' – Perpetual harmony is far from ideal. Too much stability brings stagnation. If everybody agrees with everybody about everything all the time, nothing can change – and nothing will improve. Irving Janis coined the word 'groupthink' to describe what happens when people agree too much. The group slides into a consensus, which becomes immovable. It seems to the group that they have got it right, therefore any change, by definition, is wrong. They back each other up, and frown on dissenters. This sometimes leads to catastrophe, as they are not responsive to the outside world. The world turns and turns about, but the group stays the same. The only cure for this is a dose of positive conflict.

Organisational change – Systems may stay the same just because they are there – and nobody bothers to disagree. When somebody does, it's often a revelation. Everyone realises that they've been working with glitches for years.

Productivity – Problems are ironed out more quickly when they are noticed in the early stages, rather when they have caused a situation that nobody can ignore. Where disagreement is accepted, discussions lead to rectification of mistakes before they cause any damage, and productivity improves.

CONFLICT CAN HIT THE BOTTOM LINE

Destructive conflict, on the other hand, brings with it no bonuses at all. While constructive conflict is often labelled 'cognitive' or 'co-operative' conflict, destructive conflict is often referred to as 'dysfunctional', 'affective' or 'emotional' conflict because it is driven not by ideas or opinions or the desire for solutions or by any part of the thinking brain at all, but by deep emotional responses to threatening situations. This can create in protagonists the sort of 'fight, flight or freeze' responses so important to our primeval ancestors when faced with a threat: not only deep psychological responses such as fear, anger, and aggression; but physical ones too – sweating, adrenaline rushes, raised blood pressure, nausea. Under these conditions, behaviour can become irrational, impulsive, and out of control, and the descent into destructive conflict begins.

The reasons why destructive conflict can get a hold in the workplace are numerous and are detailed in the next chapter. It can have its roots in the power structure of an organisation, the way managers handle (or fail to handle) personal or team conflicts, or a lack of fit between team goals and individual aspirations.

What many of the causes have in common is a gap between people's needs, goals or expectations and what they perceive to be the reality of the situation. What makes the conflict especially destructive is when these gaps are not recognised at an early stage and attempts made to manage them.

The danger is that if left to fester, destructive conflict can have a disastrous effect on the bottom line, as:

- people begin to focus on scoring points, rather than on finding a solution

- it creates an atmosphere of blame where people are fearful about offering new ideas

- it leads to secrecy, so important information is not made available to all who need it

- negative politics get a hold, where personalities are more important than issues

- it wastes time

- it can lead to litigation, which is extremely expensive, in money, time, and emotion.

So is destructive conflict in the workplace becoming more common, or does it just feel like it? Certainly, conflict is more likely when people feel insecure, and these days there are many reasons to feel insecure. Rapid change in technology means people are becoming de-skilled and have to keep renewing their expertise. Organisational change means more companies are being restructured and jobs are disappearing. The rules keep changing, and some people feel they just do not know where they are. If they feel out of control of their own destiny, they may feel hostile to those around them.

We are also being faced with more and more challenges to the status quo. We have a workforce of increasing diversity, which means people are working closely together who would once never even have met. The old boy network, where everyone had more or less the same background, experience and expectations, has gone for good. Now we rightly encourage people to push forward, be part of the team, and say what they think. There is no security in knowing the status quo – it will change tomorrow.

And, of course, there is more competition for business – and this is growing on a global scale. If the competition copes with change better than we do, we are lost. Change brings discomfort, loss and conflict, and we have to cope with that too.

STATISTICS

There have been few attempts to measure the prevalence of destructive conflict in UK workplaces. Those that have, have tended to concentrate on specific problems, mainly bullying – and if these are anything to go by, then it seems that destructive conflict is indeed a force to be reckoned with.

A study of 3,500 UK workers by *Mercer Human Resource Consulting* in 2002 found that more than one in five respondents had been 'bullied at work' at least once during the previous year.

Almost one in ten reported bullying on more than one occasion, with 2 per cent saying they had been bullied five or six times. The survey found bullying was prevalent at all levels of organisations: 24 per cent of middle managers and 17 per cent of senior managers said they had been bullied, suggesting just how entrenched the problem may be. Gender, age, and the size of the employer did not seem to be a factor in whether someone was bullied, though unsurprisingly, the industry they worked in did – public healthcare was the worst offending sector and retail the least.

These findings are not out of line with the large academic study carried out in 2000 by Helge Hoel and Cary Cooper for the Manchester School of Management at the University of Manchester Institute of Science and Technology (UMIST).

The researchers used two ways of measuring the extent of bullying. The first was to ask respondents if they had been bullied at work in the previous six months, using the following definition: 'A situation where one or several individuals persistently over a period of time perceive themselves to be on the receiving end of negative actions from one or several persons, in a situation where the target of bullying has difficulty in defending him or herself against these actions.' The definition did not include one-off actions.

From this, the researchers concluded that 10.6 per cent of respondents had been bullied in the previous six months. Approximately a quarter reported they had been bullied in the previous five years, with 46.5 per cent of respondents saying they had observed or witnessed bullying taking place within this period.

The second approach of Hoel and Cooper was to list a set of 'negative behaviours' and ask respondents to report their experience of these. They included:

- 'Work-related behaviours' such as persistent criticism of work, attempts to find fault, excessive monitoring, and being ignored or facing hostility when you approach someone;

- 'Personal harassment' such as insulting or offensive remarks about the person, spreading of rumours, teasing, exclusion and racism;

- 'Organisational harassment' such as having key areas of responsibility removed, being given impossible deadlines, being transferred against one's will, or being required to carry out tasks outside the job description; and

- 'Intimidation' – threats of violence, intimidating behaviour such as finger pointing, shoving or invasion of personal space, and being shouted or raged at.

Using this approach, the UMIST study found that 38 per cent of respondents had experienced at least one negative act on a weekly or more frequent basis within the last six months. Nearly a quarter had experienced two or more on a regular basis, and 16 per cent could say yes to three or more. The most frequently complained of behaviours were:

	Occasionally	Regularly
Someone withholding information which affects performance	54.0%	13.3%
Having your opinions and views ignored	49.3%	7.8%
Being given unreasonable or impossible targets or deadlines	42.2%	9.7%
Being exposed to an unmanageable workload	39.3%	14.6%
Being ordered to do work below your competence	35.1%	10.7%
Having key areas of responsibility removed or replaced with more trivial or unpleasant tasks	32.0%	6.1%
Having gossip spread about you	29.8%	4.1%
Being humiliated or ridiculed in connection with your work	27.8%	3.6%
Being shouted at or being the target of spontaneous anger	25.1%	4.7%

It should be remembered that 'occasional' could mean as often as monthly, and 'regularly' means either weekly or daily. If these experiences are taken as a whole, it builds up a rather unflattering vision of the average UK workplace. Five per cent of workers were shouted or raged at at least once a week, while nearly 15 per cent felt they were given an unreasonably heavy workload at least once a week. Almost 8 per cent felt their views were regularly ignored, while 13.3 per cent felt they weren't regularly given all the information they needed to do their jobs properly.

While there are well-known problems with the self-reporting of such a subjective phenomenon as bullying (one employee's bully is another's robust manager), the message is clear: many workplaces would seem to have all the ingredients of dysfunctional conflict. People are reporting in significant numbers that their needs, goals and expectations are being ignored on a fairly regular basis. This appears to be borne out by further findings in the UMIST study that bullying was strongly associated with a negative work climate, high workload and unsatisfactory relationships at work.

The UMIST and Mercer studies did much to bring the problems of bullying and confrontational management into the mainstream, to the extent that many large organisations are now including anti-bullying policies alongside those on harassment and equal opportunities – often using a broader dignity at work policy to include all these elements. The problem with this is that while harassment on grounds of sex, race, disability, sexual orientation or religion are illegal and have statutory definitions, bullying per se is not and does not. The danger, according to some commentators, is that because bullying can cover such a wide spectrum of behaviour, formal procedures hitherto reserved for serious allegations of harassment are being used to deal with complaints that essentially deal with a breakdown in relationships between management and staff or colleagues.

As HR consultant Peter McGeer put in a recent article:

> 'What many organisations need, as a means of avoiding costly, time-consuming and inevitably demoralising investigations into allegations of bullying, are mechanisms for dealing with instances where relationships between managers and their staff are breaking down.'

While growing employee dissatisfaction may be forcing organisations to face up to their lack of resources in this area, there is soon to be another imperative shaping the policies and procedures by which UK companies attempt to manage relationships at work. Over half a million people are currently experiencing work-related stress at a level they believe is making them ill, according to the Health and Safety Executive (HSE). Up to five million people feel 'very' or 'extremely' stressed at work. Negative relationships are one of the chief factors that have been identified by the HSE as contributing to damaging levels of stress in the workplace. Of course, stress could be a cause as well as an effect of destructive conflict and negative behaviours, and it is often hard to separate the two. Nevertheless, employers' duties include that of undertaking risk assessments under health and safety law to ensure that stress factors such as negative relationships are not putting employees' health at unacceptable risk.

As part of its war on stress, the HSE is currently in the midst of a project to develop management standards, which employers and enforcement agencies will eventually be able to use to decide if workplaces are organised in such a way that workers are at risk from stress (see **CHAPTER 5** for more on the employer's duties). At present, there are no firm plans to make these management standards mandatory – they are stated as being for 'guidance only' – but the HSE has said that in the future, following extensive testing and feedback from employers, it may take enforcement action under the health and safety legislation against employers who do not comply with the standards.

The particular management standard that deals with negative relationships demands that employers show that at least 65 per cent of employees indicate they are not subjected to unacceptable behaviour (such as bullying) at work; and that systems are in place locally to respond to any concerns.

The HSE says that in order to meet the management standard, organisations should aim for a 'state to be achieved' where:

- the organisation has, in place, agreed procedures to effectively prevent or quickly resolve conflict at work

- these procedures are agreed with employees and their representatives and enable employees to confidentially report any concerns they might have

- the organisation has a policy for dealing with unacceptable behaviour at work. This has been agreed with employees and their representatives

- the policy for dealing with unacceptable behaviour at work has been widely communicated in the organisation

- consideration is given to the way teams are organised to ensure they are cohesive, have a sound structure, clear leadership and objectives

- employees are encouraged to talk to their line manager, employee representative, or external provider about any behaviours that are causing them concern at work.

Individuals in teams are encouraged to be open and honest with each other and to be made aware of the penalties associated with unacceptable behaviour.

RISK ASSESSMENT

Carrying out a risk assessment for dysfunctional conflict may be broken down into five steps, based on the HSE's stress risk assessment model. These are:

1. identifying the hazards

2. identifying who might be harmed and why

3. developing an action plan

4. taking action

5. evaluating and monitoring.

The hardest of these steps is undoubtedly the first – all the other steps will flow from this. Finding out if your organisation has high levels of dysfunctional conflict will rely on a concerted and ongoing exercise in information gathering. This could start with a questionnaire on their own perceptions, obviously guaranteeing anonymity to the respondents. But designing a questionnaire that will garner intelligible, useful, actionable information is far from easy and may require expert help. Tools produced by the HSE as part of its pilot management standards project, while unproven, could be helpful here.

Other sources of information are likely to include absence rates, especially if particular departments or units have high rates suggesting possible problems; return to work interviews; exit interviews; and focus groups.

CONCLUSION

Matching problems to actions is far from a scientific process. Identifying the underlying causes of any conflict is a vital first step; ensuring managers have the support, skills and resources they need to manage conflict successfully will be vital.

CHAPTER 2 looks in detail at the most common causes of workplace conflict and how these can lead to a process of 'conflict escalation', while **CHAPTER 3** looks at the costs, both obvious and hidden, that can stem from this process. **CHAPTER 4** will look in detail at some of the danger signs that may indicate that dysfunctional conflict is a problem in your organisation.

But what this book aims to do above all else is to provide real, practical solutions. Dignity at work policies have their place in sending the message to employees that bullying and other conflict behaviours are not acceptable (see **CHAPTER 6**). But they are not enough in themselves. The real answer lies in investing the necessary time and resources in helping employees, especially managers, to be better equipped to deal with and manage conflict. Better training in conflict management; a greater concentration on emotional intelligence and interpersonal skills in management training; better access to mediation and dispute resolution procedures: these are the ways in which organisations can best rid themselves of the dysfunctional conflict that threatens the health, well-being and productivity of their workforces.

Chapter Two

The Causes of Workplace Conflict

Dave Liddell

INTRODUCTION

As highlighted in the previous chapter, workplace conflict has traditionally been viewed as dysfunctional, destructive and damaging – a generally undesirable by-product of organisational life. Nevertheless, given the increasing diversity in the labour market, an increasingly complex and ever-changing work environment, shifting attitudes to management, and changing expectations of employees and employers, workplace conflict is now an inescapable reality for every organisation regardless of size, sector or structure.

As in broader society, there are numerous causes of workplace conflict, some of which are obvious, others less so. But it is worth noting that, whatever the cause, workplace conflict can be a normal and even healthy part of every organisation.

Key point: Conflict itself is not the problem for organisations, but the way in which it is handled and managed

One reason conflict remains a major problem for many organisations is that they do not attribute the time, energy or resources to ensuring it is resolved speedily and effectively.

Conflict is at its most damaging when it is suppressed, avoided or allowed to escalate out of control. All stakeholders, particularly managers, need to understand the underlying conditions that contribute to workplace conflict in the modern workplace. Many managers, regardless of their role or position, when confronted with a conflict feel – quite naturally – anxious and poorly equipped to respond. After all, conflict resolution skills do not feature in our formal education system, yet the skills required to manage conflict are absolutely critical. So it is not surprising that some managers get it wrong. They may ignore conflict in the vain hope that it will go away or they may overreact and provide the spark that ignites a dangerous conflagration.

Although conflict is a given, it may not occur frequently. When it does it may come as a surprise and a shock. *'How could it happen here?'* In many cases it is complex and confusing. As the conflict escalates, it can transform itself and become all consuming for the players involved.

This chapter will offer a detailed examination of the many and varied causes of workplace conflict and the conditions that perpetuate its existence. It will draw upon a broad variety of workplace conflicts that the team at Total Conflict Management have experienced at first hand. In particular, it will highlight some of the main sources of conflict:

- between employees

- between management and employees

- within and between teams and departments

- across entire organisations.

The case study below illustrates the process through which conflict escalates and the many possible emotional reactions of the staff involved.

Case study

John and Sammi have been working together for six months in the Research and Development department of a small pharmaceutical company. John is Sammi's manager. One Monday, at one of their regular one-to-one meetings, Sammi raises, not for the first time, her desire to attend a specialist training course. Sammi, having prepared for today's meeting, argues it is important for her own personal and professional development as well as having benefits for the company

John, becoming agitated by the request, thinks he has explained before that the course is too expensive and specialist courses are not appropriate given the generic role Sammi has. He loses his patience in the meeting and tells Sammi she cannot go on the course and should stop 'mithering' him about it.

Sammi already had a pretty good idea what John was going to say and has prepared for his refusal. She did not, however, expect to be admonished in this way and she feels deeply hurt by John's attitude and abrasive behaviour. Sammi cannot stop her tears welling up and, before she can give John the 'satisfaction' of crying in front of him, she stands up and storms out of his office accidentally knocking a pile of papers off his desk on the way out.

As she walks out of John's office, Sammi feels deeply let down, even betrayed. The course was important, it would make her better at her job and it would benefit the whole company to have a trained epidemiologist in the R&D team. Sammi, an ambitious employee, feels her needs and her goals have been blocked without justification. She is amazed at the strength of feeling and the level of anger she is experiencing.

'Oh my God' thinks John, 'that was a nightmare, what was I supposed to say?' He feels dazed and confused by Sammi's reaction, he kicks himself for not preparing for today's meeting but he has spent the last three days getting a report ready for the inspection team. John also feels he has made his feelings known before: 'Why won't she listen to me, why is she so stubborn?'

John gets that tell-tale feeling in the pit of his stomach, his hands start to sweat and he immediately starts to think about how he can protect himself from a potentially hostile attack by Sammi. He knows she won't just sit back and take this.

Sammi, still frustrated and angry, goes to the toilet and tries to compose herself. 'What an ignorant, sexist idiot, no way is he getting away with this', she says to herself. Sammi knows she will have to take firm action to get on the course, and she feels John is blocking her. Would he have acted the same if she was a man? For the next two weeks, John dominates Sammi's thoughts.

About two weeks later, John and Sammi still haven't spoken to one another. Sammi avoids John and John tries everything he can not to be alone with Sammi. The tension in the R&D section is palpable, it is beginning to affect others members of the department who become uncomfortable being around them, as they feel their loyalties being split.

Sammi decides to approach her union representative to find out what sort of case she has against John, John on the other hand decides to approach Firzana, the Head of the R&D Department to have a 'word' about Sammi's attitude and behaviour.

Having entered the conflict zone, both parties have now decided to take a stand.

As the weeks go on, the hostility and bitterness grow. Two team meetings have been cancelled for spurious reasons and communication is poor if not non-existent. The head of department has even written a short memo to all staff laying down some 'guidelines' about working together and trying to be 'civil'. But the memo just seems to inflame Sammi and John's hostility and anger.

On one occasion, Sammi and John are in one of the labs when a sales person walks in, asking when a new drug will complete its trials. Sammi answers the rep saying it is nearly completed, but John intervenes to say the drug is not nearly completed and further tests are required. Sammi is furious that John has contradicted her in front of one of the reps. In Sammi's mind, this is typical of John's bullying tactics. Sammi swears to herself that John's days are numbered.

However, Sammi feels stuck. She feels that the head of department is clearly 'on his side'. She decides to take out a formal grievance, and approaches HR to find out how to do this. Angela, an experienced HR officer explains that the first stage would be to try and resolve the situation informally – has she spoken to John about this?

Sammi explains to Angela that John is a sexist bully and won't listen to reason. Sammi explains how badly she has been treated and how bad John is at managing her.

Two weeks later, John finds out third hand that Sammi has decided to pursue a formal grievance against him – he half expected it and is ready. He has compiled a 'dossier' relating to Sammi's poor work, her slack attitude and her general behaviour. He is ready to parry her attack with his counter attack, and he knows they are both heading for a potentially explosive situation. He is determined to win at all costs.

Six weeks later, after the investigation and after the grievance has been heard, Sammi and John are exhausted, but nothing has been proven and the grievance panel has put it all down to misunderstandings and an inter-personal conflict with 'equal responsibility on both sides'. John and Sammi are told to sort their 'differences out' and 'get back to work.' Neither John nor Sammi is satisfied with the outcome, they both feel the panel has sat on the fence. They are both still adamant they cannot work together.

After a great deal of thought, John decides to apply for another job. He feels down and frustrated, he thinks he deserved better than this and at his time of need, the company has turned its back on him. Three months later John leaves the firm to head up a small team for a multi-national pharmaceutical company. Sammi, on the other hand, never returns to work after going off with sickness due to stress and three months later moves to the South Coast to help run her parents' B&B. She never goes on her course and never goes back into pharmaceuticals.

THE VARIOUS LEVELS OF WORKPLACE CONFLICT

Conflicts exist at many different levels of any organisation. Conflict between two employees may arise from a disagreement about how to complete a particular task or a clash between their personal values, goals or expectations. Within a project team, conflict may be due to differing priorities or confusion over team roles. Conflict between two departments may stem from a breakdown in the communication flow or a divergence of formal objectives. A manager may experience conflict with his or her staff due to the way a change has been implemented or the allocation of resources or rewards.

Inevitably, many conflicts will involve unique factors that may not be covered here – no two conflicts are ever the same. Nevertheless, by the end of this chapter readers will see that many workplace conflicts:

- follow the same seven stages of escalation

- cause people to experience similar feelings and emotions

- tend to be based upon similar underlying causal factors.

Equipped with this knowledge, managers can begin to identify the root causes of workplace conflict and seek a resolution to the problems at an early stage.

Key point: The only way to be confident that we have access to all of the information relating to a specific workplace conflict is by actively listening to all points of view.

TRANSFORMING DYSFUNCTIONAL CONFLICT INTO HEALTHY DIALOGUE

Conflict becomes destructive when one protagonist's strategy includes, *or is perceived to include*, intentional or unintentional attempts to block the other side from fulfilling their goals, needs or expectations, or from having access to the resources required to achieve them.

Constructive/functional conflict	Destructive/dysfunctional conflict
Constructive conflict may also be known as co-operative conflict, cognitive conflict, rational conflict, healthy competition, debate, professional disagreement, etc.	Destructive conflict may also known as affective conflict, bullying, mobbing, intimidation, harassment, oppression, discrimination, aggression, violence, confrontation, etc.

Often people in conflict do not describe their situation as such – in fact people tend to avoid the word given its negative connotations of aggression or violence. For many it may begin as a sense that something important to them is being threatened. To an objective bystander it may be obvious the parties are in conflict; to the parties however, it may not feel like conflict at all – maybe just a feeling or an intuition. Nevertheless, over time, these feelings transform into a strong sense of loss, frustration and anger.

Unless they are dealt with, these feelings can become so strong that they manifest themselves as stress and anxiety and feelings of helplessness and loss of control. In the more severe cases, unresolved conflict can lead to psychological, emotional and physiological illness such as depression, post traumatic stress disorder and even self-harm and suicide.

FIGHT, FLIGHT, FREEZE OR FALL

The physical and psychological symptoms we associate with conflict are often summarised as the Fight, Flight, Freeze or Fall responses.

Fight— we decide to engage in force to cause the other party to freeze or flee.
Flight— we withdraw or flee from the conflict and surrender to the other side.
Freeze— we do nothing and wait to see what happens next.
Fall— we submit and yield to the other person.

These responses are thought to stem from the release of powerful chemicals such as adrenaline and cortisol, triggered by primeval survival instincts. They include emotional responses such as anger, fear, shock and confusion, as well as physical ones such as rapid breathing, sweating, a pounding heart, trembling or shaking and nausea. When we choose one of these responses, described by psychologists as 'emotional arousal', we can lose sight of the bigger picture and the environment and the people around us – with the potentially damaging effect that we become unable to empathise with the other party. These emotions can be very powerful and we may be unable to control them. They can prevent us from dealing with the situation in a sensible, rational and effective way. In this highly charged state, the conflict can take over with serious consequences for our sense of perception and reality. It is now far more likely that we will send that angry email, slam that door, swear and use inappropriate language, snap, snarl and sneer or say something that we will later come to regret. Emotional conflict locks us in and can very quickly spiral out of control.

Managers who wish to prevent this destructive impact must first understand the root causes of the conflict and then create opportunities to substitute emotional conflict with a more informative and rational form, known as cognitive or co-operative conflict. Co-operative conflict allows highly charged emotional responses to be replaced with intellectual, problem-solving ones based on debate and creative thought. This is a challenging and complicated task. This book will provide some techniques for transforming conflict and seeking an early and constructive resolution.

Key point: Conflict within the workplace is inevitable and unavoidable. For conflict to be transformed from destructive to constructive, it must be managed appropriately.

What happens when we are emotionally aroused during conflict:

- we only see in terms of black or white

- we may feel out of control

- we may feel a sense of uncertainty and dissociation

- our imagination plays tricks on us

- we may worry about a lose of power or control.

THE CAUSES AND SOURCES OF WORKPLACE CONFLICT

Within all organisations, there are many factors that can contribute to workplace conflict. These can be grouped under six separate headings:

1. Distributive factors

2. Structural/organisational factors

3. Human relations factors

4. Management factors

5. Factors arising from change

6. Economic, political and legal factors

The causes of workplace conflict can be shown as fishbones:

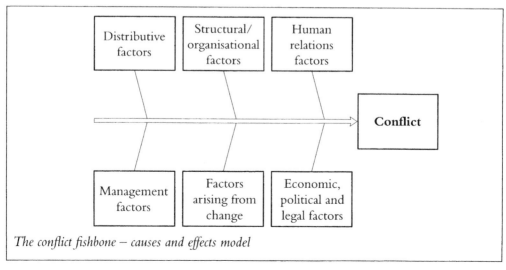

The conflict fishbone – causes and effects model

Distributive factors

Distributive conflict can arise when the rewards or resources for work are not, or are perceived not to be, distributed equally across the workforce. In a survey of over 100 organisations published by the Industrial Relations Society, in April 2001, it was discovered that 78 per cent of workplace disputes were of a distributive nature, with 40 per cent of workplace complaints being based on pay and grading, and a further 38 per cent on terms and conditions of employment.

Frequently, distributive conflict occurs in organisations where it is generally agreed that the attainment of a goal or task justifies the means taken. Unless employees have a stake in the ultimate goal, share the belief that the ends justify the means, have access to the resources to achieve the goal and enjoy their share of the rewards when the task is achieved, they begin to perceive inequalities and feel a sense of unfairness because their underlying goals and needs have not been met. In many cases, this perception of inequality and unfairness can lead to frustration and conflict at different levels of the organisation:

- between employees, groups of employees, teams and departments who are forced to compete for a finite level of resources

- between employees and management where employees feel unfairly treated.

Distributive conflict can escalate at an alarming rate and may lead to collective action in cases where a group of employees perceives it is not being given access to appropriate resources or rewards. The costs of distributive conflict can be high and the repercussions can often be felt in the organisation for many years. In many cases, distributive conflict results in:

- a gradual or sudden erosion of respect between key stakeholder groups

- an inward facing organisation which is responding reactively to internal conflict rather than responding proactively to a changing competitive environment

- a lack of trust between key stakeholder groups across the organisation, often resulting in a culture of blame

- dwindling staff morale and increasing levels of workplace stress and associated staff sickness

- high staff turnover and a haemorrhaging of core skills and competencies from the organisation, undermining competitive advantage

- increasing levels of internal competition with a direct impact upon organisational effectiveness.

Ultimately, distributive conflict can cause psychological, emotional and physiological harm for individuals whilst creating an environment in which the competition for resources regularly manifests itself as destructive conflict, discord and bullying.

Structural/organisational factors

Organisation structure can be defined as the pattern of relationships among positions in the organisation and among members of the organisation. The purpose of structure is the division of work among members of the organisation, and the co-ordination of their activities so that they are directed towards achieving the same goals and objectives. To reduce conflict, organisations need to adopt structures which facilitate people working together towards shared goals. Focusing on its component parts, structure defines tasks and responsibilities, work roles and relationships, and channels of communication. Structural factors include the specific characteristics of an organisation. There are four distinct organisational structures, each of which has its own idiosyncrasies with regard to workplace conflict:

1. **Functional structure**

   Major functions are grouped together e.g. personnel, finance, R&D etc. Within functional structures organisations may experience greater levels of sectional interest which can lead to competition and potentially destructive conflict.

   A web design company have had a major client for over six years. The sales team know the client well and often do 'loss leader' work such as back-end database updates between large contracts to maintain a good relationship. However the accounts department have told the sales team to start charging this work out as it is taking up increasing amounts of time and resources. The sales team are expecting a new contract in two months and don't want to lose the client. The potential for conflict exists where the goals between the two functions compete or have not been clearly communicated.

2. **Product/service structure**

   In larger organisations, the structure is defined by the services provided or the products manufactured. The advantages of this type of structure are that there is increased diversification and greater adaptability to the needs of customers. On the other hand, the organisation may experience conflict between service areas. This may be known as the silo effect where the left hand of the organisation doesn't know what the right hand is doing. At worst, the result is that one function gets pitted against another, at best, there is a lack of communication and co-operation.

3. **Divisional structure**

In these organisations the structure can be functional or product/service based. However, divisional structures tend to relate to a larger organisation which has a head office with smaller divisional units. In the case of multi-nationals these can be domestic or overseas. The potential for workplace conflict lies in the complexity of the organisational structure, barriers to effective communication between units, cultural differences and patterns of work, impersonal policies and practices, a perception of HQ command and control functions, lack of a clearly defined or shared vision and an increasing risk of conflict arising from competitiveness between units.

4. **Matrix team–working structures**

Matrix structures draw people together across functions, divisions or service/product areas to form a team of people who will focus on the achievement of a specific task. Matrix structures can improve cohesion, co-operation and communication for the achievement of a shared goal. Matrix structures have benefits in terms of innovation and enhanced team working and synergy. In relation to destructive workplace conflict however, matrix structures are prone to conflict when:

- communication and reporting pathways are unclear between functional and service managers

- team roles clash and personality differences turn into inter–personal conflict

- there is unresolved divergence in the objectives of the team

- inflexible or inequitable reward systems cause jealousies and conflict or

- there is personal antipathy to team working.

It is impossible to identify any one form of structure as having a particular predisposition to destructive conflict over another. However, there are distinct factors that may causes conflict to be more prevalent within one structure than another. The following table compares those structural factors that can cause or perpetuate workplace conflict and those structural factors that can reduce the potential for it.

Structures that can cause or perpetuate conflict	Structures that can reduce conflict
Rigid and inflexible structures which are slow to respond to employees' changing needs.	Flexible structures which can respond to the changing needs of the workforce.
Overly hierarchical structures with several levels of management which can block communication and innovation. Rigid hierarchical bureaucracies can impede the kind of integration, collaboration, communication and flexibility that are essential for responding to change. They are often inefficient.	Flatter structures emphasise the horizontal links between parts of organisations, enabling liaisons and partnerships across disciplines and departments. Flatter structures reduce the barriers between managers and staff and make for more clear and rapid decision-making.
Complex organisations in which employees are unclear about roles, responsibilities and reporting structures.	Simple structures in which the reporting and delegation arrangements are clear and unambiguous.
A structure in which the expectations of employees' freedom and dignity at work are out of line with the controls the employer feels are necessary to maintain authority.	A structure in which a shared vision is communicated and developed, and transformational leadership enables a common understanding between managers and employees.
Imposed mechanistic approaches to strategy formulation with little involvement of internal stakeholders.	Organic and informal approaches in which internal stakeholders engage in strategy formulation and have a sense of common purpose and ownership over the direction of the organisation.
An over-reliance on technological means of communication such as email, on informal systems such as the grapevine, or on ad hoc systems such as occasional briefings.	Use of various media to enable effective communication with the emphasis on face-to-face communication with well defined feedback and review mechanisms.

Human relations factors

Mirroring society as a whole, organisations are complex systems comprising a diverse and broad range of individuals whose backgrounds, perceptions, values, roles, beliefs, cultures, attitudes, opinions, needs, goals, expectations and behaviours are interwoven and inter-related. The following model shows how the experiences we have had, our interactions with others within the workplace, and our expectations of the future link to make us the individuals we are.

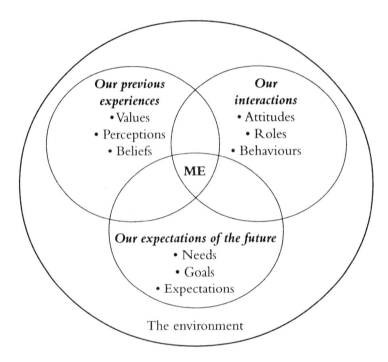

Individual conflict-influencing factors

At an individual level these factors can sometimes clash or compete, causing conflicts and discord. To others, this may appear to be a mundane personality clash, and, in the early stages of conflict escalation may appear petty and silly – except in the eyes of the protagonists, for whom the conflict is potentially stressful and traumatic.

At the early stages of conflict escalation, as parties enter the 'conflict zone' and begin to take a stand, (see **PAGE 30** The stages of conflict escalation) the clashes can often be resolved amicably through dialogue and discussion. However, if this does not happen or it fails, the opportunity to transform the conflict may be lost. The parties are then left with little more than their primitive responses to conflict – fight, flight, freeze or fall.

Below are just a few of the many causes of human relations conflict:

- a clash of personalities, values, beliefs etc

- misunderstandings about a particular issue

- jealousy and envy leading to personal attacks, sniping and vindictiveness

- isolating people from other group members

- blaming people or persistently criticising them

- prejudicial, racist, sexist or inappropriate language.

Examples of some of the causes of workplace conflict

Conflicting needs

Two members of staff work opposite one another. One needs to use the telephone to contact clients while the other needs to use the computer to compile reports and letters. The employee on the telephone has a loud voice and laugh and disturbs the other. In response the other person plays his Oasis CD to drown out the sound so he can concentrate. The situation quickly deteriorates until neither person is talking to the other nor prepared to adjust their working practices to accommodate the other person's needs.

Conflicting styles

Two staff work together in a small charity. One worker works best in a very structured environment while the other works best in an unstructured environment. These two workers soon drive each other crazy as they constantly work in conflict with one another and do not learn to accept one another's work style.

Conflicting perceptions

Two staff work on the front desk of a large GP's surgery. The Surgery Manager decides to recruit a receptionist to meet and greet patients as they arrive. One member of staff sees the new recruit as an advantage (one more set of hands to get the job done), while another sees her as a personal insult (a message that the existing staff are not performing adequately).

Conflict within teams

A team of 15 works in a large university department. It has been asked to agree a business plan for the coming three years and has identified an internal facilitator to help agree the plan. However, on the day of the meeting, three of the more senior members of the team arrive with a completed plan and bound copies for all staff team members. They explain to the facilitator that they have devised the plan and wish to use it as a model. The rest of the team were unaware that this was happening and two members voice their disquiet. After a very heated debate in which aggressive and confrontational language is used, the facilitator tries to intervene to get the day back on track. However, at this stage, two team members leave in disgust, four are left bickering and two of the newer members look bemused and upset. The business plan is never written and the department is absorbed into a larger school six months later.

Why do people get into conflict?

Human relations conflict often exists because the parties are, quite naturally, different people. Destructive conflict arises when individuals focus on the differences to draw conclusions, make assumptions and perpetuate prejudices about others. Co-operative conflict provides opportunities to learn from one another, to listen to one another and to share our experiences. Destructive conflict tears people apart and focuses on what separates us, not what brings us together.

At a wider level, organisational diversity policies and an emerging legislative framework have sought to tackle many of the inequalities within the workplace. However, diversity and personal differences still provide opportunities for some to launch attacks or undermine other team members. We all abhor the team bully who abuses their position of power to attempt to gain an unfair advantage over another. This form of conflict, be it driven by gender, ethnic, religious, cultural, physical or sexual differences, is unwelcome and harmful. Individuals may feel victimised and unfairly treated – they may begin to feel isolated, vulnerable and frustrated. Rather than using diversity as a strength and an opportunity to seek mutually acceptable and creative solutions to new and emerging problems, teams becomes fragmented, they experience high levels of stress and they become inward facing and unproductive.

> In a study of over 500 employees from 70 UK organisations in 2000, Manchester School of Management at UMIST found that 10.5% or one in ten people had been bullied at work in the past six months.
>
> *Hoel H and Cooper C, Destructive Conflict and Bullying at Work UMIST, April 2000*

If left unresolved, such conflicts will have a significant impact on the psychological, emotional and physiological well-being of employees and managers. This is perhaps the least visible and most commonly overlooked form of workplace conflict – it can be subtle, insidious and hard to identify. It may be mistakenly written off as office banter or letting off steam. Team leaders and managers need to explore ways of responding to human relations conflicts swiftly and robustly and agree boundaries which make it clear that the language of destructive conflict is not acceptable in the office.

Management factors

Some conflicts are caused by the specific actions, or inactions, of managers within the organisation.

There has been a marked shift in the UK away from a production-orientated approach towards a market-orientated provision of services. Managers have had to become increasingly aware of the nature of the external marketplace as well as adopt a new form of enlightened, innovative and visionary style of leadership for their staff. In some cases, this has resulted in a shift in emphasis from autocratic approaches, where managers hold the power and essentially instruct their staff, to more consultative, participatory and democratic styles where managers share the decision-making process with their staff. As a result, managers have been required to develop new skills in leadership, coaching, facilitation, communication, problem-solving and mediation.

In response, some managers have adopted styles and approaches that allow them to relate to staff in empathic and intuitive ways, often focusing on the emotional as well as the practical responses to a particular problem or issue. Others have found the transition confusing and complicated.

Whatever their response, managers facing an increasingly complex and challenging series of pressures often report they feel stuck between 'a rock and a hard place' when it comes to managing differences in values, goals, needs or expectations among staff. Some are able to recognise the importance of their role in managing the diversity within their teams, applying principles of fairness and dignity in the way they make decisions and allocate tasks and offering stimulating rewards for performance and productivity. For these managers the driving factors are:

Fairness, dignity, honesty

Perhaps most importantly, some managers have learned to confront conflict and to seek a constructive and productive resolution through open, honest and authentic dialogue.

In some cases however, the fear of confronting conflict leads to a lack of involvement by managers – they ignore it and hope it will go away or they try to manage it from a distance. This can leave teams and individuals feeling isolated, confused and unsupported. Communication becomes difficult and issues that could be resolved quickly fester and grow. Conflict avoidance can mean the difference between an early resolution and a process of escalation resulting in significant and costly harm.

Below are some of the situations in which managers may experience conflict:

- intervening in inter-personal and inter-group conflicts

- giving 'bad news' including redundancies or budget cuts

- managing poor performance, absence and sickness

- facilitating difficult meetings

- challenging inappropriate behaviour in the office.

Every manager will experience conflict at some time in his or her career. Indeed, even the most experienced and competent managers can struggle to respond – sometimes, their attempts fail and their efforts are in vain. Yet, regardless of the outcome, conflict provides an opportunity for all managers and their staff to learn and grow.

Managers who:

- view conflict as a positive and healthy sign of working life

- understand their own and their teams' conflict styles

- remain disinterested and don't get drawn into conflict

- recognise the root causes of conflict and how it escalates

- apply practical approaches to resolving conflict

- take responsibility for creating a climate of trust, dignity and fairness…

…are the managers who tend to have the greatest success.

As this book highlights, the stakes are very high for managers. As a result, many are concerned that workplace conflict is a symptom that they are not coping with effectively. They may seek to suppress, defer or ignore conflict in the hope it won't be noticed or will go away. This not only negates their role but also deprives them of opportunities to resolve the issue. Consequently, the conflict escalates and requires significant remedial action once it can no longer be concealed.

Factors arising from change

The speed of organisational change offers all enterprises great opportunities to grow, adapt and develop new competitive advantages. In these cases change may provide:

- access to new technologies leading to innovation and product/service enhancement

- faster production, speeding up the time it takes to get a product or service to market

- increasing information about the needs of the market enabling faster and more effective decision-making

- changing working practices enabling organisations to have access to a more diverse and flexible workforce.

All of the above bring potential advantages and benefits to organisations. However, in some cases, change happens so rapidly that many employees are left feeling overcome and bewildered. Changing structures, new work processes and additional procedures challenge employees' beliefs about their own identity and values within the workplace. They may experience feelings of disorientation, insecurity and uncertainty. Employees tend to display a variety of emotional reactions to management decisions and behaviours. They may feel the change has deprived them of a known way of life and security, and cast uncertain shadows on their careers. Of course, many employees welcome change with open arms and thrive on it; others may perceive it as a threat, something to be resisted, believing it will have a negative impact on them, their needs and their goals. Consequently, they do not engage in the process or its outcome, with the result that conflict emerges and manifests itself as resistance to change.

Against this backdrop, the very individuals who should be acting as a force for change may resist it. Individuals form alliances with like-minded individuals and as time goes on, the change is potentially stalled and hindered as cliques and factions emerge. Faced with increasing pressure and stress, change agents and managers may respond in one of two ways: either by abandoning the change or by forcing it through. Both responses will lead to an escalation of destructive conflict and may quickly turn into a serious and potentially collective dispute.

Change and conflict are inextricably linked and when both are managed effectively, the results can be productive, constructive and sustainable. When managed inappropriately, the outcomes include increased competition, stress, anxiety, bitter rivalries, jealousies and confusion – add into this the use or misuse of power by the change agent and there now exists the perfect catalyst for dysfunctional workplace conflict.

Economic, political and technological factors

Economic factors which can impact upon workplace conflict include:

- fluctuating levels of employment

- labour market demand

- rate of inflation

- differences in pay between occupations and across occupations

- distributive factors and inequality of access to resources and rewards.

At an individual level, economic factors may not appear to have a significant impact. However, when organisations are experiencing financial difficulty due to economic downturn, deregulation, a merger or acquisition or increased competition, there is a strong likelihood that employees, teams and departments will be required to compete more aggressively. Coupled to this there may be a significant risk of redundancy, down-sizing and changes to working practices to cut costs quickly, increase sales and improve productivity.

In this economic climate, fear, mistrust and anxiety may come to the fore. Stress will result with a direct impact upon personal relations. In these circumstances, conflict can emerge with quite devastating consequences.

According to the 1998 Workplace Employee Relations Survey (WERS), the percentage of British firms experiencing some form of collective action fell from 13 per cent to 2 per cent of workplaces between 1990 and 1998, and strike action fell from 11 per cent to 1 per cent. Non-strike action fell from 5 to 1 per cent. But the percentage of firms being involved in Industrial Tribunals rose from 9 per cent to 13 per cent (1990 to 1998). As the authors of the WERS note: 'In short, individual conflict between employers and employees rose during the course of our series (of surveys) at the same time that collective conflict all but disappeared.'

Since 1997 there has been a proliferation of rules and legislation focusing on workers' rights and the promotion of 'fairness at work'. This has led many organisations to amend their working practices. In particular, many firms have seen the emergence of workplace partnerships between management and trade unions, politically motivated to reduce the incidence of collective disputes and to enable stability, growth and enhanced employee relations.

The aims of workplace partnerships are to:

- encourage a joint commitment to the success of the organisation

- enhance efforts to build trust and attempt to address the issue of employment security in exchange for flexibility

- improve the provision of quality training programmes

- engage managers and employees together in information-sharing and joint problem-solving.

Meanwhile the fairness at work agenda has raised awareness of inequalities in the workplace and the existence of phenomena such as the 'sticky floor' and the 'glass ceiling'. It has also provided a framework for organisations to resolve disputes in legislation such as the Employment Rights (Dispute Resolution) Act 1998 and the more recent Employment Act 2002, with the intrinsic commitment to the internal resolution of workplace disputes.

While much has been done to reduce the incidence and effects of collective disputes, far more is required to reduce the damage caused by individual conflicts within the workplace.

THE SEVEN STAGES OF CONFLICT ESCALATION

Most workplace conflicts follow similar patterns of escalation. During the escalation process, parties may experience some or all of the following stages. There is no set timescale for the process. For instance some disputes may never get beyond stage one, rumbling on for years without seeming to get worse. In a road rage incident, on the other hand, the conflict can escalate through the seven stages in the blink of an eye.

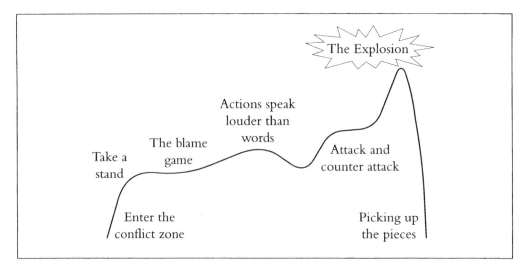

1. Entering the 'conflict zone'

As parties enter the conflict zone, divergence between one or more of their needs, goals or expectations begin to emerge. This leads to a sense of frustration and anxiety and the early warning signs may include reduced communication, hostility, inappropriate behaviours and attempts to isolate the other. The parties adopt a series of positions to communicate their own points of view, which can become mutually exclusive and seemingly irreconcilable. This adds to the frustration, anger and sense of mistrust for all parties as their positions are not accepted. Frequently at this stage, the parties lose sight of common ground and focus on the factors that have driven them apart.

Resolving differences at this early stage and encouraging the parties to let off steam, step back and talk it through can be very valuable. By engaging the parties in a process of open and honest dialogue, positions can be softened, behaviours changed, attitudes realigned and dialogue developed. However, many managers miss this vital opportunity to nip conflict in the bud, leaving it to fester so it requires only a spark to ignite it, and throw all parties into a destructive spiral of stressful and damaging attack and counter attack.

Key point: One of the main factors in destructive workplace conflict is avoiding it at the early stages in the hope it will go away.

2. Taking a stand

The parties are immersed in the conflict zone. Though they may still be prepared to engage in dialogue, if their efforts to seek a resolution are fruitless, they will start to doubt that a solution can be found and they will question the 'reasonableness' of the other party. As the conflict escalates and rational communication is replaced with emotional confrontation, the parties may become more forceful in their positions. The focus is now on winning.

At this stage, the protagonists may try to forge alliances with people they believe will support and strengthen their position. Inflexibility and stubbornness become the staple diet of the conflict and tactics may appear confused, irrational and increasingly aggressive. These behaviours however, reflect the parties' perceptions of reality – their 'truth'. In conflict, our sense of the 'truth' is extremely powerful, and any attempts to force parties to accept another 'truth' may be viewed with suspicion. It is hard for parties to listen while they are planning their strategy, and their ability to empathise is seriously undermined.

3. The blame game

As the conflict escalates, the parties' tactics are aimed at gaining and maintaining the upper hand. Both parties are convinced they are in the right and that the threat to their values, needs, goals or expectations is real and substantial. The language of blame becomes the language of the conflict ...

> 'You should back down ... you are wrong.'
> 'They always behave like this and should be punished.'
> 'If it wasn't for them ...'
> 'You're the manager, you do something about them ...'

This language presents the other party as the wrong-doer and is designed to influence decision-makers. It can become increasingly threatening, sometimes even aggressive and violent. The parties are being driven by their emotional responses and may experience symptoms of stress and anxiety. They may try to project an image of righteousness and strength while absolving themselves of responsibility for the conflict. The blame game prevents protagonists from looking inward and maintains an unhealthy focus on the tactics and games being played. Any reasonable attempt to engage the parties in communication may result in bickering, arguments and hostility. It is unusual for either party in a conflict to win the blame game.

4. Actions speak louder than words

Not unsurprisingly, as the conflict escalates, the communication and dialogue trail off with the parties beginning to feel further debate is unlikely to resolve anything. The parties develop strategies that will make the other side back down and yield to their demands – they aim to block the opposition from attaining their needs, goals and expectations while enabling their own to be met. As the communication process fades into distant memory, it is replaced with a series of non-verbal signals and actions. The protagonists form stereotypical views of their counterparts based on assumptions and prejudice. Typically these are wholly inaccurate but they are used to rationalise and justify their own behaviour and activities. Tactics include:

- drovoking the other person to act in a particular way

- trading insults and negative comments

- preventing the other party from accessing information, files, records etc

- issuing threats and ultimata.

5. Attack – counter attack

These threats and ultimata become increasingly rigid and inflexible. As the conflict continues, the parties start to view each other as almost sub-human. They react violently to one another and may experience high levels of anxiety in each other's presence. Given the codes and norms of the workplace, it probably won't be easy for them to engage in open hostility, so the attacks and counter attacks become increasingly subversive and devious.

The parties may start to feel out of control and their alliances begin to fail as the conflict becomes more serious and threatening. They may lose sight of their strategy and begin to demand immediate actions from their counterparts, some of which will leave them with little room for manoeuvre. If it hadn't already, the conflict will now have taken over and the parties will be entirely locked in. To back down now would end in a loss of face, submission and failure.

At this stage, the parties may seek external assistance, sometimes as a tactic to strengthen their position, sometimes as a genuine cry for help and support.

6. The explosion

This is the most dangerous of the stages. Threats and ultimata have come and gone and the parties now come to blows. At this stage, the fight or flight response is extremely powerful and the basis of the parties' activities is survival at all costs. In the workplace the parties are at war. The smallest spark could result in an all out offensive and the normal rules of engagement have been tossed in the bin. The parties engage in often brutal and increasingly desperate attacks and seek to inflict as much damage on the other as possible. They will seek to damage their opponent's reputation, integrity, power base and alliances. They may lash out blindly and may even seek to inflict damage on other staff, managers, representatives, mediators or negotiators.

As the conflict grows in intensity and sucks other people in, the pressure increases and the parties experience extreme levels of stress. It may explode at any time. The conflict will now be potentially highly dangerous with very little consideration of personal needs; it is about winning at any cost. This can have a number of outcomes, including both parties being subjected to disciplinary action, one or both parties pursuing grievances, one or both parties being dismissed, a criminal investigation, or litigation by the parties or the organisation.

7. Picking up the pieces

Whether or not both parties survive the explosion, it is left to others to help pick up the pieces. The only concern now is to restore the peace and get the team back on track. Handled well and with dignity and fairness, this stage can lead to a positive period of reflection, dialogue, change, growth and learning. If it is ignored or handled badly, however, the pieces may litter the workplace for many years to come. Managers should be encouraged to adopt an impartial, facilitative approach. Acting as mediators, they can agree boundaries and ground rules which will enable the parties to talk and listen.

CONFLICT HANDLING STYLES AND THEIR IMPACT ON WORKPLACE CONFLICT

Studies into human responses to conflict have shown that individuals react to such situations in a variety of different ways. These responses are based upon the importance that we place upon our own goals and the value that we place on our relationship with the other person. We may have a variety of conflict management styles, however it is common to apply one or two dominant styles when we are faced with workplace conflict. These responses, which may be allocated animal names, are based five conflict management styles:

1. avoidance

2. forcing

3. smoothing

4. compromising

5. collaborating.

Conflict management styles

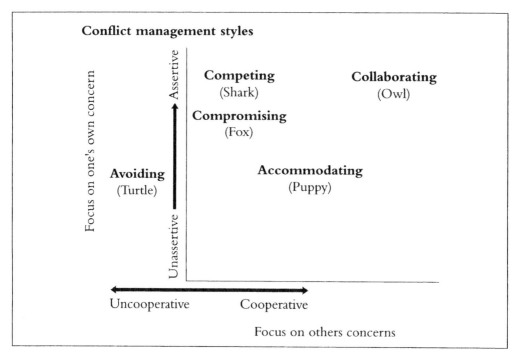

Let us consider each one in more detail.

The Turtle (Avoiding) – Withdraws from conflict and avoids it in the hope it will go away. In doing so turtles may appear to be timid or passive. They appear to give up their own goals and do little to maintain a positive relationship with the other person. This can be seen as a sign of weakness and can lead to frustration and a sense of helplessness. Turtles may lack credibility and can create frustration in others. In certain circumstances, turtles have been known to snap and metamorphose into sharks.

The Shark (Forcing) – Forces its own goals and tries to control others. Sharks don't care who loses as long as it is not them. Sharks may use their power and influence to 'get the job done' but often pay the price over the longer term. Sharks see losing as a failure and see failure as a sign of weakness. By forcing their goals on others, sharks are often seen by others as controlling, intimidating and hostile.

The Puppy (Smoothing) – Tries to accommodate all points of view, is deeply concerned about its relationship with others and does little to achieve its own goals. Can be seen as trying too hard to maintain a relationship. When they are in the middle of a conflict, puppies get confused and can often frustrate parties who are looking for a stronger and more robust perspective.

The Fox (Compromising) – Foxes can see the value in negotiation and are prepared to give up some of their goals to maintain a positive relationship. They tend to look for a safe and constructive working environment. However, they may feel they are giving something up to secure peace, and this sense of loss can lead to frustration, sometimes forcing them into more shark-like behaviours. Hence they run the risk of being viewed as inconsistent.

The Owl (Collaborating) – Thrives on mutual dialogue and collaboration and views conflict as an opportunity to grow and learn. Owls consider all points of view; they value both their own goals and their relationships with others. They see conflict as a constructive opportunity to engage in joint problem-solving aimed at a mutually acceptable and satisfactory outcome, and to develop constructive and sustainable relationships. Owls are committed to the principles of 'I win – you win'.

Chapter Three

The Costs of Conflict

Marion McCrindle

INTRODUCTION

For many people organisational conflict is characterised by strikes and picket lines. Vivid images of the miners' strike is the classic definition for those over thirty, while more recent images may be fire-fighters round a brazier or London Underground workers threatening to withdraw service at Christmas and on New Year's Eve. However, most organisational conflict remains internal. It can be the result of simple causes, such as poor communication, or complex causes, involving a range of factors. It can be systemic or localised, a permanent feature or transient.

Organisational conflict is also experienced at a personal level. Many employees have seen or experienced bullying and stress – personal, eroding forms of workplace conflict – but conflict can arise from personal style and manner as well as individual belief and conduct.

The 'cost' of each form of conflict can be measured in both human and financial terms. The easily identifiable costs are those that arise directly: in a transport dispute, for example, lost revenues is the imputed value of running the service for a day that is lost when employees go on strike; similarly, an award at Tribunal is highly visible, as is the legal bill which invariably accompanies it. However, even in such cases the true cost of the conflict is more complex. Many elements are only identified over time and involve concepts such as trust, reputation and allegiance.

At a personal level the true cost of bullying or stress goes well beyond any legal costs: the cost to the individual, the team, and ultimately to the organisation are more difficult to pin down.

Some of the costs dealt with in this chapter lean heavily on assumptions and none can be definitive. Many organisations see conflict as an inevitable part of working life: spending time costing repercussions that do not have an immediate effect on the bottom line is seen as wasted activity. For those who would like to know more, the cost of conflict is not easily defined. Take the public health arguments about the benefits of investing in health promotion: these often stumble when calculations are sought of actual future savings. The same concept is often applied in organisations – if you can't quantify it, it isn't worth knowing.

This chapter seeks to challenge that belief. It looks at some of the very real, yet often hidden costs of conflict for an organisation. It finds that the true cost of conflict – while it can never be pinned down exactly – is enormous.

THE 'HEADLINE' FIGURES

Newspaper headlines emblazon huge sums of money lost to the economy as the result of national industrial unrest: one dispute at British Airways was cited as costing £125 million[1]. We read that at the level of the individual, the Health and Safety Executive estimates that bullying costs employers 80 million lost working days and up to £2 billion in lost revenue each year[2]. Many studies indicate that 30 to 40 per cent of a manager's day-to-day activity involves dealing with some form of conflict. On this basis, a quick (and simplistic) costing is easy: the cost of conflict to an executive earning £60K per annum is between £18 and £24K per annum (plus on-costs). Multiply this by the number of executives in your organisation and you have the baseline cost of conflict.

This grabs our attention – a major objective – and gives us easily remembered figures to quote in conversations with friends and colleagues. But we rarely see the calculation methodologies for these huge sums. Some look straightforward:

- number of days' absence in the year

- number of days lost × average salary cost (or highest salary cost?)

- number of days lost × average sales per day + cost of recovery

- cost of recovery = number of days of reduced production × (full production – actual production) + number of additional hours worked required to recover the situation x average salary costs (often at overtime rate).

But how accurate are they, how all embracing? Whilst the number of noughts quoted clearly indicates some rounding up, the basis of the calculation remains at the visible level; the 'invisible' (personal) can often cost more.

What is the 'cost' of conflict within service industries, for example? Disruption to a bank would differ from disruption to a hospital. The availability of alternative supply would be a significant factor here – customers could change banks, while choosing an alternative hospital is not yet a possibility in most parts of the country. The financial cost of a dispute in a bank would therefore be much higher, but the human cost of a hospital dispute could clearly be more extreme, as could the political damage. It is consideration of these factors which leads to the regular debate about strike bans in the public sector – as well as actual bans in the police force and army.

The other cost a company might wish to avoid is the reputation damage of a complaint at tribunal or in court – the newspaper headline cost. A decision to defend or settle out of court often starts with, 'What is it going to cost?' and a pragmatic decision is taken to minimise loss. The 'cost' of such a conflict is seen as financial – tangible and quantifiable. Offering an appeasement sum to an employee who claims victimisation or discrimination may well be the more pragmatic alternative to going to court and running up huge legal bills, and less damaging – it keeps the company out of the papers and managers out of court.

But there are other costs which are often ignored. These include the impact on:

- the rest of the team – other employees

- management – who may not feel supported and hence might start to feel aggrieved in turn

- the employee in dispute, who may start to suspect a cover up or who may think, 'That was easy!' and be encouraged to try another claim.

In short, the costs of conflict do not cease to accrue once the 'dispute' is over, as was well illustrated in the industrial dispute between the Patrick Stevedores and the Maritime Union of Australia (MUA), details of which hit the headlines over a period of weeks in 1998.

At the heart of this dispute lay the belief of the MUA that the government planned to remove them from the waterfront: this stemmed in part from a leaked government brief which noted their intention of making the waterfront more cost effective. By removing the MUA the government would be seen as controlling industrial relations which, in turn, would enhance their ability to influence relations in other sectors.

A web article on the dispute by Gowri Paramanathan[3] examines the costs involved: the headings provide a useful checklist for organisations.

- 'financial and legal – compensation to the wharfies, loss of sales (due to non-operating workforce), court fees'

- 'industrial – a revolution of working practices took places as a direct result in terms of the abolition of double shifts, the introduction of annualised salaries, reduction of manning levels'

    Industrial costs mean different things according to where the observer is standing. The man who invented the Spinning Jenny and those of other forward-thinking inventors probably looked at the benefits their inventions brought to their fellow workers – release from dirt, danger and tedium; the ability to work faster. However some fellow workers would have found it threatening in terms of change. The employers would have seen only benefits (as long as the set-up costs could be recouped quickly).

- 'social costs – the company has now invested in robot technology to improve productivity, Australia's trading reputation was damaged by the waterfront industrial dispute, causing problems for other businesses.'

    The social cost can mean a slight change of practice to one man but a completely new way of looking at work and the human role within it to another. Whilst perhaps viewed as positive by employers – and perhaps employees too in the long-term – the immediate effect of each aspect of change after the stevedore dispute could well have been seen as a loss – particularly if they were the vehicles by which the employees gained their salary levels and concomitant standard of living. Other 'costs' to organised labour were the loss of union power as the employers gain new flexibilities and loss of jobs (reduced manning levels), both aspects of the human cost of conflict. There was also a change to the social pattern of work with the introduction of robots and to the waterfront (types of business).

- 'political costs – the government gained a negative image among the working class, though productivity gains were achieved which had a positive impact on the economy.'

    The 'political' costs can be defined in a global sense as the impact of the event on the fortunes of the government or the organisation: but there is also an internal interpretation whereby the politics of an organisation refers to the way it works in terms of how decisions get made, the relationships which influence the direction of the organisation – who is listened to, who has no influence – and the balance of power between different individuals and groups. The changes which any dispute gives rise to are often described as 'cost' or 'benefits' according to how it feels for the employees involved. In this example, the 'cost' of the dispute in global political terms was that the government lost the confidence of the people through their handling of the situation, even though financially the economy improved.

At an organisational level no future waterside dispute would be handled that way: the cost was high thus different strategies would need to be devised. Also, the shareholders would need to be courted as they would now ask many more questions about management's ability to manage their workforce. Parallels with other headline British industry conflicts resound such as the mining and car industries. But if each organisation/industry involved in conflict calculated the 'cost' under these headings – along with those used elsewhere in this chapter – then the costs could be better forecast and the implication of events better understood.

Area of cost	Organisational interpretation	Issues for our organisation
Financial/ legal	Is this going to hit the bottom line? Is there a financial repercussion/a legal dimension? – cost of litigation or risk to reputation?	
Industrial	Impact on working practice.	
Social	Impact on work organisation (job design, team structures, competencies, training needs etc.).	
Political	Are there any political ramifications? Are there any internal political considerations? Where does this leave us in terms of the future?	

THE REPUTATION 'COST'

As far as the employer is concerned, there are at least two types of reputation at stake: first, a reputation as a sound company to do business with or as a reliable provider of services (in terms of quality, quantity, price consistency, dialogue with customers); and, second, a reputation as a 'good' employer (in terms of equity and fairness). Sometimes the two areas are linked but usually customers concern themselves with the former and workers (current or potential) with the latter.

Many companies will make large out-of-court settlements to avoid damage to their reputation or image – irrespective of the truth of the accusations; others go to court or employment tribunals regardless of the effect on their reputation – either because they believe they are right and want to take a stand, or because they do not realise the message the case will give.

Imagine that Megabucks Bank is taken to tribunal by a female employee claiming it has failed to pay her a large bonus she thinks was due on contractual grounds. The bank contests this: its defence is strident and the image it paints of the employee is very poor. However, the employee wins her case. The stories in the tabloids are lurid and the culture of the bank laid bare. What effect might this have on the organisation's reputation?

Who will be 'interested'? This is likely to affect employees and potential employees more than customers because it is an employment issue and does not affect service – unless, of course, this was a key account manager who made exceptional returns, or hers was one of a series of high claims that was affecting shareholder confidence.

What are the 'costs'? Apart from the obvious cost of the payment and the legal cost, the potential costs are:

- **The impact it has on other employees' productivity.** If the litigant leaves, there are implications for morale and motivation among the remaining workforce – who's likely to be next? Will anyone else want to make a similar claim? Are female employees thinking about how the company treated that employee and losing confidence in Megabucks as an employer?

- **The impact on employee retention.** Will more employees leave as a result of this?

- **The impact on recruitment.** Will recruitment of good quality female employees drop as a result?

- **Potential concern from shareholders.** An increasing number of investors monitor equal opportunity issues and may be embarrassed by the bank's stance and behaviour – they might place more demands on the bank (cost of satisfying their queries) or, in extremis, leave and take accounts with them.

To measure the potential costs to the business of such a case, the bank might monitor:

- the number of accounts held/closed overall or in the immediately following quarter

- the number of accounts held/closed by female customers overall or in the immediately following quarter

- the number of accounts opened in the following quarter – up or down? Are these high or low earning accounts? Is the ratio of male/female the same?

These are quantifiable, but it would be difficult to determine what percentage was due to the Tribunal case and what percentage was due to other factors. If a company wanted to measure this it might consider:

- conducting telephone interviews with customers who closed accounts

- hiring a consultancy to conduct a market confidence survey (i.e. phoning a number of individuals/companies asking why they did not open accounts with the company

- following up any job applicants who subsequently withdrew

- asking a headhunting company to canvas a number of potential applicants on their database to gauge perceptions of the company in the recruitment marketplace etc.

However it would be most unusual to find employers attempting to measure these factors because:

- it might be seen as acknowledging there was a problem (though that might be overcome if the organisation is known for its learning culture and keenness to avoid repetition of mistakes)

- it would be an additional cost

- many factors in employee and customer choice are unpredictable

- it would prolong an unpleasant experience: the best thing would be seen as putting it behind them and moving on.

In this instance the full 'cost' of conflict in terms of reputation is unlikely to be explored in depth by Megabucks: indeed, it is likely to be slight, both in terms of any lasting or damaging effect. Whilst some potential employees might be put off applying, other personal motivators will have a strong pull. If the company is otherwise known as a strong player in the particular field of business – giving good operational experience and offering good rewards – then its attraction will remain, perhaps even be augmented for those with more strident tendencies. In this situation the bank would need to be careful it did not start to recruit in an image it did not want to nurture.

In other circumstances, were the organisation to be seen as a poor employer then the 'cost' will be high as recruitment, retention, productivity and output become affected.

Another aspect to this is that of the reputation of the *individual*. Where a female has a string of operational successes, a court case against a company will not dent her reputation: there have been several high profile cases to substantiate this in recent years. But other women might suffer – either from the personal trauma of having to go through the court and the attendant publicity or because of loss of reputation in operational circles – sometimes earning them the name of a trouble-maker.

The impact of this would depend on how closely the organisations kept in contact with each other. In close-knit business communities anyone going to court/Tribunal can earn the label of trouble-maker and, despite some potential legal remedies in the areas of discrimination, some individuals become blacklisted. For the less confident, less qualified person, the risk of being blacklisted if they complain persists and this is likely to remain a deterrent.

Thus the actual 'cost' of loss of reputation needs to be calculated on a sliding scale, reviewing all the possible repercussions, calculating a likelihood (or weighting) percentage and then multiplying them by the potential cost.

Where there is little customer choice – e.g. a local hospital is obliged to pay a huge sum of money for negligence following an error in the birth of a baby – the cost of lost reputation is more one of confidence and relationships between employees and the public. Where there is a choice – e.g. disputes in transport services – we may see the public lose confidence but they only vote with their feet where there is a viable alternative. But they often become more vocal in respect of complaints[4] so there may be the added cost of administrative/ management time as well as potential cost of compensation.

In the case of a charity, loss of reputation can be particularly serious – because if income is lost not only does the organisation suffer but so do those who benefited from their activity. A recent headline read:

> 'One of Britain's best known charities has descended into fresh turmoil. Details leaked from an RSPCA council meeting last week paint a picture of a deeply divided organisation, facing a grassroots revolt and a financial crisis [over] News that the animal charity is entrenched in a bitter row over plans to cut £8m in costs …'[5]

If such an organisation loses the confidence of the public there are many 'customers' who will suffer, though as many alternative organisations who may benefit.

THE LEGAL 'COST'

The easy one to identify is the solicitors' bill. The forgotten ones can include:

- Management/employee time spent on paperwork and going to court and giving evidence (which can lead to subsequent absence).

- The emotional costs to managers and employees of being involved in the case, which can lead to subsequent absence.

- The trigger for subsequent claims – from the same or other employees who perceive they too have a claim or who may simply try it on.

- The increasing temptation in dealing with all future issues (let alone disputes) to consult lawyers 'just in case' – this can border on dependency and lead to a very high tariff.

Alternatives to acquiring legal costs include seeking mediation. A recent article in *People Management* notes that in a recent poll of barristers and solicitors specialising in employment law, 'one member replied that a case settled in one day of mediation had saved the expense of a 10-day trial'[6].

Whilst some employees will demand their day in court, if mediation could be built into disciplinary/grievance policies and become part of the organisation's culture, it has the potential to save a lot of money (see **CHAPTER 6**). There is a growing trend to establish mediation skills within organisations: training programmes are available from ACAS as well as private providers, though what consideration is given to on-going support for the mediators is not clear[7].

THE COMPANY/CUSTOMER 'COST'

In the most public arena of conflict – the strike – the key element of the relationship between a company and its customers is one of trust. In the 1987 dispute at British Telecom walkout of the engineers did not lead to the predicted widespread collapse of the telephone network as the systems no longer relied on human intervention and some of the managers went into the exchanges. The system carried on unaffected, thus the dispute remained one between employer and employee: the customer was simply a bystander.

In a dispute at British Airways, where baggage handlers walked out over a holiday weekend, while customers were clearly not happy at the disruption to their travel, what made them angry with BA was a lack of communication – about what was happening, when they would leave and so on. But to what extent would that affect future sales? If the issue is seen as a problem that is common to the wider industry, the impact of any one incident on a company is diluted. If it is seen as specific to that company – and worse, at a particular time of year – then alternative supply (of departure and destination location, comfort, price, service etc.) and the degree of customer satisfaction overall will determine the impact.

Conflict affects the level of sales of a company where:

- there is a threat to continuity of distribution either in the course of the dispute, or from future disputes

- prices rise as a result of extra costs being passed on directly

- an alternative appears which offers less risk for the same cost or at a cost the customer is happy to accept

- in a personal dispute with a key sales/account manager, some customers move with that manager when he/she goes to a company offering a similar service.

There is a long list of rogue factors in the decision to find alternative sources of supply, but one way of finding out is to ask the customer directly. Again some may give a range of reasons or fog, but a company could learn a lot by asking questions – as long as the reason is to learn rather than to defend.

In the case of London Underground, while their very public disputes over a range of topics greatly inconvenience and anger a lot of their customers, there are few viable options – especially with the introduction of the congestion charge as well as high parking costs in London. So while numbers may drop a little, the conflict does not have a significant impact on overall sales[8]. Fears about safety have a greater impact.

However, the development of technology means fewer large companies are immune from the 'no alternative' argument. A good example is the Post Office. For years the labour intensive nature of the service – together with government support for a monopoly position – meant customers had no viable alternatives during disputes. Only in large conurbations were viable alternatives used – van or bicycle delivery across cities or within confined areas. Once the dispute was over many of the new services disappeared as the costs could not be justified.

However, as technology has developed and the use of electronic mail becomes far more widespread – as well as providing a satisfactory legal alternative to fax – disputes do not have the same impact. Customers have lost much of their confidence and see the new services as equally reliable. Also the gradual erosion of the monopoly makes the establishment of alternative services more viable economically. Remote homes will continue to depend on a universal provider for service at a reasonable cost. The debate as to which has accelerated the current situation more effectively – conflict within the Post Office or the development of technology – is the stuff of dinner conversation or exam papers, but whichever is deemed the more accountable, conflict has played its role and ultimately those who will pay are those who caused it, if the loss of the monopoly means the company down-sizing even further.

A relatively new area in the literature on company/customer cost is that of violence against employees as a result of dissatisfaction with the service being provided. A very vivid example is the increasing violence against clinical staff in UK hospitals and paramedics attending call-outs for ambulance assistance. Others include attacks on transport staff and government officials in housing offices. The 'cost' to the organisation includes absence, injury allowance under employment and health and safety laws as well as liability under the laws governing vicarious liability.

The Health and Safety Executive notes on its website that violent incidents at work have increased since 1997 by 5 per cent, though they consider this is understating the number, as many incidents do not get reported:

> 'Physical attacks are obviously dangerous, but serious or persistent verbal abuse can be a significant problem too, as it can cause damage to employees' health through anxiety and stress. For their employers this can represent a real financial cost – through low staff morale and high staff

turnover. This in turn can affect the confidence of a business and its profitability. Further costs may arise from expensive insurance premiums and compensation payments.'

Indeed there is now a specialist body, the Institute of Conflict Management, dedicated to setting national standards in the prevention and management of conflict and aggression to employees.

THE EMPLOYER/EMPLOYEE RELATIONSHIP 'COST'

Of far more immediate impact on the bottom line is the cost of internal conflict – between employer and employee[9]. Employment Tribunal applications rose between 1999 and 2000 but have consistently fallen since, reaching 98,617 in 2002–2003. In 2002–2003 payouts at Tribunal for unfair dismissal and sex, disability and race discrimination alone cost UK employers £24 million.

Many organisations are increasingly encouraging employees to identify themselves with the success of the company, with the use of incentives such as share schemes and profit-related pay. Workers' councils have not been successfully introduced in the UK, a result of reluctance on both sides, and many directors shy away from recognising unions unless their organisation meets the legal recognition requirements. The philosophy for many remains that unions cause conflict and conflict costs money.

Yet collective action is less common now – though 2003 saw a rising number of strikes. This is partly due to the amount of UK legislation curbing collective demonstration, but it also reflects the change in the size and scope of trade unions. In 1983 there were 456 unions; by 2001 this had fallen to 276. Similarly in 1983 TU membership was 11.7 million; by 2001 this had fallen to 7.8 million.

Strikes are more costly to organise now, mainly because of the legal requirements. Employees have seen poor results from collective action, so only those industries with high density union membership remain open to significant challenge (e.g. transport, postal services etc.): the opportunity cost of lost wages is higher than it used to be.

Taking a case to Tribunal is a relatively low-cost option to the employee as wages continue to be received while any action is pursued. Similarly the cost of pursuing a union-backed case against an employer through the Tribunal system is often a means of receiving a higher benefit. For an employer, if the conflict is with an employee who can claim discrimination, the cost of that conflict is potentially without a ceiling[10].

Another major aspect of the employer/employee relationship is the more personal aspect – between manager and member of staff and between colleagues. Typical indications of conflict at work in this respect include increased absence, lower productivity and higher labour turnover.

Two of the most common reasons for personal conflict at work are bullying and stress. In an article entitled, 'The hidden costs of having a bully on the balance sheet', Tim Field notes[11]:

> 'In the majority of cases, the bullying that comes to light is only the tip of an iceberg of wrongdoing. From lying on their CV to falsifying the circumstances around the departure from their previous job, the serial bully is almost always misappropriating budgets, leaking confidential information, breaching rules and regulations and codes of conduct whilst making false claims about their own work and achievements. Indiscretion, maladministration, malpractice and negligence are also common. But often, glib, superficial charm combined with an exceptional verbal facility ensure that the serial bully is able to talk their way out of every corner.'

Stress-related legal claims have increased significantly, with many factors thought to be at play. Conflict at work can lead to more accidents as employees take less care and some forms of stress can lead to clinical mental illness. At worst, it can lead to death or suicide. In turn this can lead to claims for negligence and higher insurance premiums.

In terms of calculating the employee-related costs of conflict, a manager can look at:

- the time spent on resolving grievances, disputes and disciplinaries

- the time spent negotiating and meeting with unions/staff representative on issues of actual or potential conflict

- average number of tribunal/court cases in the previous five years, noting any trends

- time spent preparing documentation and attending briefings for Tribunals/court

- time spent in Tribunals/courts

- cost of awards and representation

- cost of any personal injury awards.

THE MOTIVATION 'COST'

Motivation covers both the way in which something is tackled (in this context, the way a task or role is carried out), and the personal reasons we do things and why we do them in a particular way. While creative conflict can be highly motivating for some people, most find negative conflict disruptive, and, at worst, destructive.

In his 1970s book, Bateson[12] outlines five categories of factors which influence our motivation: our sense of identity, our beliefs and values, our capabilities, our behaviour norms and our appreciation of our environment. The cost of affecting one of these areas is high – both for managers and employees. At a simple level, the cost of denying an issue that an individual feels expresses their identity is much more significant – and hence is likely to have further reaching consequences – than denying an issue to do with their environment. The difficulty is that unless you have spent time getting to know that individual – presuming they are conscious of their motivation and are willing to share some of their thinking with you – you do not know which issues will affect them.

Let us take a simple aspect of social conflict: the seating arrangement in a small office. It is important to understand whether it is an identity issue or an environment issue for each individual. This is not a common language thus many employees will only know that things matter more or less to them. If sitting next to the window is an issue of status, then to be asked to sit somewhere further away is not merely a question of light but a status issue. If the employee is status-conscious, or at least has a view of their own status in relation to someone else's, the conflict will be much more serious than for someone who is not – who may not even realise it could be seen that way.

Managers need to be aware that even the simplest changes can have significant implications. In day-to-day management, if they are not aware of the individual motivation of their staff, the cost will be high in terms of energy required to deal with the individual(s) and in handling the effect of that loss of motivation on the work of the team. Managers will need training and support in this regard.

In terms of approaching a task, reduced motivation can 'cost' the organisation in each of the categories in this chapter. In extreme cases:

- complaints to the press can result in a loss of reputation

- service to customers can suffer

- employees can become more obstructive, litigious, and as a result, legal costs could be incurred

- lack of motivation can seek some physical outlet – slower working/ sabotage/lack of incentive to seek better ways of working or reduced quality, hence productivity can fall

- absence almost inevitably increases – from accidents or sickness with all the related costs – as does the rate at which people leave the organisation, leading to more recruitment activity and cost.

Thus motivation is a major factor in the management of conflict and managers need far more understanding of the psychology of the workplace if they are to succeed in the current organisational climate.

THE PRODUCTIVITY 'COST'

Productivity, where measured, is normally assessed in terms of physical output per employee, team or shift. As noted above, where motivation is reduced, output and productivity can be reduced too; in extreme cases sabotage or theft can result. Thus any change to productivity should be investigated – to learn the reasons why.

As well as simply noting productivity levels, managers should monitor the variances as symptoms of possible changes in motivation. Lowered productivity could indicate stress, bullying, a motivation problem, a team problem, a training need, reduced confidence etc. Thus where productivity has fallen the following checklist might be useful:

Issues to be considered	Questions to ask	Areas for action
Staffing levels. Has absence increased/ decreased?	What are the causes? Are absence levels on a par with last period? This time last year? Consistent with other movements in the industry sector/ local area?	In-house data. There could be local environment issues: check with Public Health/local papers. Could improved technology assist?
Number of staffing issues/ grievances	Are there any grievances? If so, how does the number compare with last period/quarter/ other work areas/other managers? Are there any informal staffing issues?	Seek advice from HR. If such data not held consider starting to do so. Are there any training needs? Would a 360° review be useful/suitable?
Turnover	Are levels consistent with previous periods/year-on-year figures? Are any reasons for variance known?	Seek advice from HR. If such data not held consider starting to do so.
Deliberate acts	What is the likelihood of sabotage taking place/theft, including stealing of secrets?	Audit and probe any inconsistencies.
Environmental factors	Have there been any changes that could influence productivity?	Undertake a risk assessment/audit and probe any inconsistencies.

THE ABSENTEE 'COST'

In 2002 sickness absence cost British Industry £11.6 billion. An average of 8.9 working days were lost across all industries, at a cost of £637 per employee (2002) in the public sector and £466 per employee in the private sector. Overall, 166 million days were lost through absence in 2002.

Whilst much of the absence was due to genuine illness, a percentage was due to 'other factors'. The actual level varies from organisation to organisation. Established reasons employees are more likely to absent themselves from the work environment include:

- boredom, low morale, job dissatisfaction, high pressure/stress, poor work environment, poor ratio of staff to workload, lack of teamwork, poor leadership

- being employed in a large organisation

- working in a routine job with no pressure to meet deadlines

- working in an organisation (or department) that tolerates high absence or provides sick leave as part of the contract.

The first of these lists factors that are all associated with conflict. As noted above, where there is conflict in an organisation, employees are more likely to lose motivation and an inevitable outcome of this is that some will absent themselves from the workplace. The number that do this will vary according to their relationship with their manager – the quality of leadership – the quality of absence management and the degree to which there are other avenues of support (counselling services, occupational health services, etc.).

Having a policy of self-certification for each absence can be useful in terms of providing information. If you are concerned about the impact of conflict in your organisation, monitor absence levels across each work area and ask yourself the following questions:

- Are absence levels higher or lower than the previous quarter/this time last year?

- What are the reasons given for absence?

- Is the pattern different from usual?

- Do managers carry out return-to-work interviews? If so, what have they been finding out? If not, why not? Is this a training need or does policy need tightening?

- Has there been a rise in the number of grievances/complaints in the organisation?

- Does any particular manager have higher than average levels of absence in their department? Does this coincide with more HR issues? Is there a training need? Is any bullying taking place?

To cost absence, take the salary and on-cost of each absent employee; add any replacement costs incurred. Calculate a sliding scale of likelihood i.e. if 50 per cent of the absence were not genuine the cost would be £x: if just 10 per cent were not genuine the cost would be £y. The actual percentage could be gauged on the information gleaned from return-to-work interviews.

THE TURNOVER 'COST'

Employees both leave and stay with organisations for a number of reasons. While exit interviews can be useful in determining why staff are leaving, they cannot be relied upon. Rather they are indicative. Certainly discontent in the workplace is a common reason for leaving, though rarely without other factors co-existing:

- Find out the average labour turnover rate for your industry.

- Measure this against your rate of turnover: is this the same as last quarter/this time last year?

- Check any exit data: examine the reasons for leaving. In the light of findings are your policies adequate and well-communicated?
  An organisation found several female employees leaving because they could not cope with the conflict of balancing work and motherhood: they were unaware there was a policy on work-life balance and that moving to part-time hours was an option. Digging further, the organisation found their line manager did not approve of part-time working so had not told the women of the policy at the time it was introduced. The organisation then changed its communication strategy regarding changes to policies.

- Determine any differences in the local labour market and any recent changes (new businesses coming into the area? Are they offering training/high wages?).

- Examine the turnover data by work area – could higher turnover in one area indicate weak management/bullying? – and level.

- Investigate the areas highlighted by your findings.

A significant tranche of turnover costs derive from anther type of conflict – that of lack of work-life balance. Conflict occurs when the combined pressures from work and home make it difficult to meet the demands of either role. Stress can come from either domain and the potential for work-life conflict increases when heavy job demands are coupled with low control; when supervisors are not sensitive to employee needs; and when long work hours or inflexible work schedules conflict with family commitments or childcare arrangements. Employees experiencing high levels of conflict tend to miss work more often than others, spend more unproductive time at work, and ultimately, may seek work elsewhere or exit the labour force. Such consequences indicate that work-life conflict is costly to organisations and costly to individuals in terms of personal, economic and social well-being.

David Clutterbuck, who has recently published a book on work-life balance, notes:

> 'Conflict between work and non-work lives doesn't take place in a vacuum. It takes place in a complicated environment in which difficult choices are the norm. Work/work conflict (what tasks to do, and what tasks to stop doing) is as much of a problem for most organisations and individuals as work/non-work conflict; the volume of choice and the range of opportunities expand daily'[13].

Organisations that ignore this conflict risk high turnover and increased costs of recruitment.

Thus the areas which employers need to examine and consider are:

- opportunities to work flexibly: (this can mean a more flexible approach to hours of work, place of work): working from home; hot desking – this is clearly easier in some industries than others but involve employees in the decision by asking them to show you how the work could be done if they only worked the hours they wish to (in the workplace); job-sharing; annualised hours

- improvement of turnover rates; average or below local market conditions

- ensuring employees feel they are treated with dignity and respect

- acknowledgement of the staff contribution to the organisation

- ensuring employees feel supported and able to challenge discriminatory behaviours

- reduction of grievances and disciplinary action

- ensuring employees feel safe at work

- ensuring communication in the workplace is effective

- sharing information about the organisation and its progress

- ensuring recruitment procedures are transparent

- reduction of long working hours

- making appropriate training/development available (including literacy, numeracy, language training and NVQs for employees without qualifications)

- supporting employees with caring responsibilities

- conducting a survey whereby employees are able to express their views on a number of topics selected by the employer.

THE RECRUITMENT 'COST'

Just as many companies look at the cost of replacing someone as the cost of the recruiting company/the advert/time taken to select them and perhaps their induction training, so the cost of conflict within companies is not well documented. The cost of recruitment is often simply seen as the cost of the advertising agency (very often a percentage between 12.5 and 50 per cent of the total remuneration package plus travel, subsistence and VAT). This sometimes excludes the cost of advertising, the hire of any venue as an assessment centre or for interviewing purposes, assessment tools – which can include the design cost if they are work based tests – catering or candidates' expenses. Some companies structure recruitment fee payment as a third on accepting the assignment, a third on presentation of a shortlist and a third on appointment: in the case of early termination of the assignment others charge a day rate for each day of consultancy (plus VAT and travel) for work undertaken to date.

According to the state of the economy, the salary offered, the reputation of the company, the challenge of the job etc. there is no certainty that posts can be filled. Even where agencies use their own databank and engage in an extensive search, some posts remain difficult to fill. Costs continue to accrue at each separate search.

Even where a company undertakes its own recruitment there are costs:

- physical costs such as advertising, postage (if packs of literature are sent out), telephone/email costs (though the latter are often hidden)

- management time in agreeing to recruit – this can include Board involvement – preparing the job description and person specification; answering phone queries (where allowed); shortlisting; interviewing

- administrative time in preparing letters and sending them out; dealing with telephone calls; printing out any email correspondence on the subject; preparing interview packs; arranging accommodation; ensuring appropriate catering is arranged and available on the day; meeting candidates and taking them to the interview room; sending out offer/rejection letters; arranging contracts

- opportunity costs of all aspects of the above.

Then there is the cost of induction: something that should be seen as the final stage of recruitment rather than an add-on. If an organisation does not get this right the new member of staff may well leave and the cost of recruitment is doubled. Yet often induction is extremely brief and fails to communicate simple things like:

- how the telephone system works

- the culture of the organisation[14]

- who makes the decisions and what the processes are to get them made; the management structures for operational strategy etc.

- a quick guide round the intranet – how to get the more recent information quickly, etc.

There are several model induction checklists on the web e.g. **http://www.newcastle.edu.au/services/hrm/induction/shortterm/check lists/casual_induction_staffmember.htm** The notion of having a checklist which the new employee completes as the induction programme is rolled out is one all organisations should consider[15]. It gives employees a good picture of what the organisation regards as essential to know and provides a sound discussion document to introduce them to the culture of the organisation i.e. explaining why each element is important. Its completion also becomes a tool they can use if any elements are not provided in a timely fashion.

It has often been said that if staff were told what behaviours were and were not acceptable at the recruitment stage, then bullying would be greatly reduced. Regrettably there is no research on this, but organisations could certainly tackle bullying more confidently if they had such obvious cultural definition.

CONCLUSION

The costs associated with conflict should receive broad definition and calculation. Whilst most conflicts would benefit from an individual balance sheet approach – a cost-benefit analysis – overriding human factors will usually prevail. These can have a disproportionate effect on the final calculations – both positively and negatively – and results will vary from individual to individual, organisation to organisation and industry to industry.

Whilst some costs are more readily identifiable and can be directly addressed such as those of absenteeism, turnover and poor performance arising from bullying, others are more complex and require more analysis and multi-faceted handling. Managers may not need to become cost accountants but they do need to develop the ability to see conflict in the round and hone their interpersonal knowledge and skills so that the negative aspects are minimised and the creative aspects released.

REFERENCES

1   Walsh, J. 'BA clears the air with trade union', *People Management*, 20 January 2000, pp 14–15.
2   Allan, Anna, 'Dignity at Work' (a book review), *People Management*, 20 November 2003, p 53.
3   **http://www.boredofstudies.org/courses/arts/business/2001_BusStud_A_Case_Study_MUA_Gowri.pdf**
4   The imbalance of power is one reason for having a regulator – someone to whom the 'little' individual can complain.
5   Guardian Unlimited – 'Animal charity plunges into conflict' (13 May 2003).
6   Raymond Jeffers, 'A problem shared ...', *People Management*, 18 December 2003, p 17. Ironically the same article cites one of the factors holding back the use of mediation was the possible additional costs.
7   One NHS Trust supports its mediators with professional supervision. ACAS is piloting a mediation service to companies employing less than 50 employees in Yorkshire and the Humber region and East London.
8   Conversely, after a major accident, travellers do seek alternative forms of transport (e.g. from the railway network post Hatfield).
9   Dan Dana, who runs the Mediation Training Institute International and who has written extensively on the subject of conflict, notes that in the US an estimated 65 per cent of performance problems 'result from strained relationships between employees, not from

deficits in individual employees' skill or motivation'. At **http://www.mediation works.com** he offers a free download of a chapter from his book, *Managing Differences: How to Build Better Relationships at Work and Home* and an on-line calculator for the cost of conflict at **http://www.hrtools.com/Frames.asp?Category=5&Toolkit=25&Process =1006**.

10 In 2002–2003 the maximum award for race discrimination was £814,877: ETS Annual Report and Accounts, p 26.

11 *Accounting for Business*, 1 February 2002.

12 Bateson, G. *Steps to an Ecology of Mind*, Balantine Books, New York 1972.

13 Clutterbuck D, 'Not Flexible Enough', *People Management*, 2003 (web article). Currently the NHS is pursuing a multi-stage award, Improving Working Lives (IWL), whereby each Trust must be able to demonstrate that its staff believe and are happy with the organisation's commitment to working with their staff to improve their work-life balance. Increasingly constructed like Investors in People, every Trust is obliged to attain accreditation by a set date: failure to do so will affect the overall performance rating of that Trust and in turn its star ratings, which directly affects its freedom to operate. IWL is seen as essential to the NHS' ability to recruit and retain their staff.

14 A London based organisation's experience is that a third of staff who leave have less than one year's service: they have pinpointed that the major problem is induction.

15 There are now bodies which can accredit induction programmes towards awards e.g. within the recruitment industry.

Chapter Four
Recognising the Danger Signs

Diane Hall

INTRODUCTION

Bullying and harassment is now recognised as an increasing problem in today's workplace and is attracting considerable media attention. One of the most high profile recent cases has been that of Steven Horkulak, a City worker who was awarded nearly a million pounds in damages after claiming that the president of his employers, Cantor Fitzgerald International, had screamed obscenities at him and threatened him over a period of six months.

But bullying has been reported in many other places too. Bullying and harassment in a north Devon Council was said to have become endemic, with intimidation, swearing, ridicule and discourtesy by a few members being identified as serious issues. Bullying in the NHS has been the subject of a number of media reports with nurses complaining of constant criticism, humiliation, being shouted at or marginalised by their managers. A report claimed that thousands of junior doctors are regularly subjected to bullying. There have also been reports of bullying of teachers by head teachers, parents and governors, and the types of bullying include unfair criticism, being shouted at and the withholding of information.

How does an organisation or manager recognise that bullying is taking place? What are the danger signs and how may problems be prevented? This chapter will begin by discussing some common definitions of bullying and harassment, and then go on to give examples of bullying behaviours and discuss the difference between strong management and bullying. It will also discuss the subjective nature of bullying, describe the main psychological and physical signs that someone is being bullied, explain how to identify vulnerable individuals and groups and finally outline some ways of preventing and reducing problems.

DEFINING WORKPLACE BULLYING AND HARASSMENT

There are no universally agreed definitions of workplace bullying and harassment but a discussion of the views of key institutions and those from the academic literature is given below.

Bullying

The Chartered Institute of Personnel and Development (CIPD) (2002) defines bullying as

> 'any persistent behaviour, directed against an individual, which is intimidating, offensive or malicious and which undermines the confidence and self-esteem of the recipient. Bullying is largely identified not so much by what has been done but rather by the effect it has on its target.'

The Advisory, Conciliation and Arbitration Service (ACAS) (2003) says that

> 'Bullying may be characterised as offensive, intimidating, malicious or insulting behaviour, an abuse of power through means intended to undermine, humiliate, denigrate or injure the recipient.'

The Andrea Adams Trust (one of the main UK charities working to support victims of bullying and to reduce the incidence of workplace bullying) defines bullying as:

> 'Unwarranted, offensive, humiliating, undermining behaviour towards an individual or groups of employees.
>
> Such persistently negative malicious attacks on personal or professional performance are typically unpredictable, unfair and irrational.
>
> An abuse of power or position that can cause such anxiety that people gradually lose all belief in themselves, suffering physical ill-health and mental distress as a direct result.'

Enduring negative acts in the workplace are variously described in the academic literature as mobbing (the term used in Scandinavia), petty tyranny, psychological terror, abusive supervision and emotional abuse at work. However they all refer to similar phenomena – the systematic and repeated mistreatment of a colleague or subordinate against which the victim may have difficulty defending him or herself.

A broad consensus has emerged among researchers that there are three main elements to bullying. First that it is directed towards a target; second that there is more than a single act; and third that the target ends up in an inferior position from which it is difficult to defend him or herself. The imbalance in power relationships between the parties is a key element in bullying and this view is reflected in the definitions such as those given above. It is not bullying if two parties of approximately equal strength are in conflict, although power refers not only to that gained from hierarchical position but also that from personal authority, knowledge/experience or strength of personality.

Harassment

The CIPD (2002) describes harassment as unwanted behaviour that a person finds intimidating, upsetting, embarrassing, humiliating or offensive.

Harassment, according to ACAS (2003), is unwanted conduct affecting the dignity of men and women in the workplace. Harassment differs from bullying in that it is normally linked to particular personal issues such as race, ethnic origin, sex, sexual orientation, disability, age, religious belief or HIV/AIDS. It can also be a single serious incident. ACAS sees a key element of harassment as being that the actions or comments are viewed as demeaning and unacceptable to the individual.

Acts of harassment may potentially be acts of discrimination and therefore fall within the scope of anti-discrimination legislation. The legal definitions of harassment and the law relating to discrimination are discussed in **CHAPTER 5**.

RECOGNISING INAPPROPRIATE BEHAVIOUR

Workplace bullying

Workplace bullying is essentially an aggressive act, usually involving psychological violence but sometimes minor physical aggression.

Just as there is no universally agreed definition of workplace bullying, there is no universal agreement on what constitutes bullying behaviour. In fact, because bullying depends to a large extent on the perceptions of the target, it is understandable that there is a whole range of behaviours which could be classified as bullying and that what constitutes bullying for one individual may be perfectly acceptable to another (see also the subjective nature of bullying below).

However, there is some convergence between various authors and institutions on what constitutes bullying behaviour. **TABLE 1** shows a comparison of the sorts of behaviours viewed as bullying from four sources. The first is from a comprehensive study of destructive conflict and bullying at work in Britain by the University of Manchester Institute of Science and Technology (UMIST) (Hoel and Cooper, 2000). Analysing responses from more than 5,000 individuals in more than 70 organisations, the authors identified nine negative behaviours that were most frequently encountered. The second source is the CIPD and the third ACAS. The final source is the Andrea Adams Trust.

From the Table it is evident that there is a very wide range of behaviours that might be considered bullying. Examples include persistent and unjust criticism, humiliating and offensive remarks, being ignored or 'sent to Coventry', imposing menial tasks and setting someone up to fail. Minor physical aggression may include intimidating behaviour such as finger-pointing and invasion of personal space as well as threats of violence. Many bullying behaviours relate to how an individual is managed or supervised. In fact, there is considerable evidence that bullying is associated with poor management. For example in the UMIST study, Hoel and Cooper (2000) found that in nearly 75 per cent of bullying incidents, managers or those in superior positions were reported as perpetrators. They also found that the experiences of bullying were, in the main, linked with four negative management or leadership styles which were identified as autocratic, divisive, laissez-faire, and non-contingent punishment (where punishment seems unrelated to the subordinate's behaviour). In contrast, they found that environments which were relatively bullying-free were linked with three positive management styles: participative leadership, integrity, and individual consideration. Bullying behaviours at higher levels in an organisation may be so subtle and insidious that they are not at all easy to recognise.

The use of bullying behaviour by managers to achieve the unfair removal of an individual from their post has been identified by both the Andrea Adams Trust and Bully OnLine (the website of the UK National Workplace Bullying Advisory Line). The Andrea Adams Trust says the bully looks for any reason to accuse their target of poor performance in order to bring about their dismissal. This has been echoed by a number of trade unions who have argued that some bullying managers look to fabricate a case of poor performance in order to dismiss an employee rather than make a redundancy payment. Bully OnLine takes this view further by suggesting that unjustified disciplinary action on trivial or specious charges, attempted dismissal on fabricated charges or flimsy excuses, coercion to resign, enforced redundancy, ill health or early retirement are all bullying behaviours.

Examples of Bullying Behaviours

UMIST STUDY OF DESTRUCTIVE CONFLICT & BULLYING AT WORK (NINE MOST FREQUENT NEGATIVE BEHAVIOURS)	CHARTERED INSTITUTE OF PERSONNEL & DEVELOPMENT	ADVISORY, CONCILIATION SERVICE (ACAS)	ANDREA ADAMS TRUST
	Persistent negative comments		
	Unjustified persistent criticism	Constant criticism	Persistent criticism
	Monitoring work unnecessarily and intrusively	Overbearing supervision or other misuse of power or position	
		Making comments about job security without foundation	
	Picking on one person for criticism when there is a common problem	Unfair treatment	
	Imposing unfair sanctions		Dispensing unfair punishment out of the blue
		Copying memos that are critical about someone to others who do not need to know	
Being humiliated or ridiculed in connection with your work	Humiliating someone in front of others Offensive or abusive personal remarks	Ridiculing or demeaning someone	Public humiliation Personal insults and name calling
Spreading gossip		Spreading malicious rumours	
Having your opinions and views ignored	Ostracism	Exclusion or victimisation	Being overruled, ignored, marginalised or excluded
	Making false allegations Belittling someone's opinion		
Having key areas of responsibility removed or replaced with more trivial or unpleasant tasks	Removing areas of responsibility without justification		Increasing responsibility whilst decreasing authority Removing areas of responsibility

Examples of Bullying Behaviours—Continued

UMIST STUDY OF DESTRUCTIVE CONFLICT & BULLYING AT WORK (9 MOST FREQUENT NEGATIVE BEHAVIOURS)	CHARTERED INSTITUTE OF PERSONNEL & DEVELOPMENT	ADVISORY, CONCILIATION SERVICE (ACAS)	ANDREA ADAMS TRUST
Being ordered to do work below your competence			Imposing menial tasks
Being given tasks with unreasonable or impossible deadlines	Setting unattainable targets		Setting unrealistic deadlines for an increased workload
	Constantly changing work targets in order to cause someone to fail	Setting someone up to fail	Constantly changing targets or work guidelines Setting someone up to fail
Being exposed to an unmanageable workload		Deliberately undermining a competent worker by overloading	Setting tasks the target was never contracted to do
Someone withholding information which affects your performance	Reducing someone's effectiveness by withholding information		Deliberately sabotaging or impeding work performance Witholding work related information
	Not giving credit where it is due		
	Claiming credit for someone else's work Undervaluing work done		Constantly undervaluing effort
		Preventing individuals progressing by intentionally blocking promotion or training opportunities	
			Persecution through threats Persecution through fear
Being shouted at or being the target of spontaneous anger	Email threats – 'flame' mail		Repeatedly shouting or swearing in public or private

Harassment

Harassment is a form of bullying that is almost always focused on highly personal qualities such as gender, race, disability, sexual orientation, religion or belief. However, unlike bullying it often has a physical component such as touch or unwelcome contact – especially in the case of sexual harassment.

The CIPD (2002) suggest that harassment may include the following:

- Physical contact.

- Jokes, offensive language, gossip, slander, sectarian songs and letters.

- Display of posters, graffiti, obscene gestures, flags, bunting and emblems.

- Isolation or non co-operation and exclusion from social activities.

- Coercion for sexual favours and pressure to participate in religious/political groups.

- Intrusion by pestering, spying and stalking.

Employment tribunals have recognised a number of behaviours relating to gender, race and disability as harassment. For example sexual harassment can include leering at a person's body, requesting sexual favours, unwelcome contact of a sexual nature and sexual assault. Harassment can include jokes and banter, name-calling, practical jokes, unwelcome gifts, and mimicking an individual's disability.

THE DIFFERENCE BETWEEN CONSTRUCTIVE CONFLICT/STRONG MANAGEMENT AND BULLYING

As the CIPD has pointed out, legitimate, constructive and fair criticism of an employee's performance or behaviour at work is not bullying – nor is an occasional voice raised in anger. However, there are three crucial differences between constructive conflict and bullying and harassment. First, for an act to be considered bullying there must be an uneven power relationship between the protagonists, based either on hierarchical position or on strength of personality or knowledge. This imbalance must be such that the weaker party has difficulty defending him or herself. For example, a staff member could be vulnerable to bullying by their manager because of fears about their job security or of not achieving a good appraisal that may result in a loss of performance-related pay.

The second difference between constructive conflict and bullying relates to the nature of the act: whether it is directed at an individual personally and whether that person finds it threatening, offensive or demeaning. In constructive conflict, the protagonists are of roughly equal strength and the conflict is kept outside the personal arena.

The third difference relates to the persistent nature of bullying – it involves more than a single act and many surveys define bullying in terms of weekly acts over a period of at least six months. Constructive conflict is more likely to be a 'one-off' occurrence with the parties resolving their differences or agreeing to differ in a relatively short time.

It is evident, therefore, that a conflict between a manager and a member of their staff has the potential to be bullying simply because of the inherent imbalance in the power relationship. Managers need to be extremely careful that they do not engage in behaviour that could undermine or threaten the dignity of their staff, and to be sensitive enough to know when criticism moves from being legitimate to becoming personal and unfair.

THE SUBJECTIVE NATURE OF BULLYING AND HARASSMENT

Bullying is an ambiguous concept and is essentially subjective in that it relies on the perceptions of targets for definition. Incidents that are offensive to one individual may not be to another. A person who has been bullied is not a passive receiver but an:

> 'active interpreter of ambiguous stimuli from the environment who makes a choice about the way he/she reacts.' (Liefooghe & Olafsson, 1999)

Bullying is also a cultural and social phenomenon. Liefooghe & Olafsson suggest an individual draws on socially agreed representations of bullying to explain and describe their experience. Lewis (2003) emphasises the importance of social influence in creating shared beliefs and understanding about bullying and suggests that work colleagues are central to the social construction of bullying at work. It follows therefore that bullying behaviour is often context-specific and whether particular behaviour is interpreted as bullying will depend on the context in which it takes place, including the culture of the organisation and the age, ethnicity and personal characteristics of the individuals involved.

A number of authors (Cowie *et al.*, 2002) have drawn attention to the way in which the values and norms of the workplace influence how bullying is defined and how employees interpret events. Bullying needs to be understood at a number of different levels; individual, organisational and social/cultural.

As we have seen, it is the perception of the individual that is the key component in interpreting whether an act constitutes bullying or harassment. Some definitions of bullying and harassment in anti-bullying policies contain a test of 'reasonableness' which serves the purpose of putting some boundaries on the subjective nature of the acts and therefore may provide some protection from claims of particularly sensitive individuals. However the difficulty is in deciding what is 'reasonable'. For example, managers may wish to draw the boundaries of bullying behaviour narrowly, defining many forms of management pressure on subordinates as legitimate. Subordinates, on the other hand (especially if they are not able to complain in other ways), may wish to widen the boundaries to limit the scope for management pressure.

Blame

Organisations often treat the victim of bullying as the problem, accepting the prejudices produced by the offenders and blaming the victims for the situation in which they find themselves. This can lead to the victim, not the offender, being seen as the trouble-maker and eventually the one who is forced out of the organisation.

Attribution theory has been seen as useful in explaining some aspects of bullying. Findings from attribution studies suggest that individuals tend to project the reasons for positive experiences towards themselves and for negative experiences towards others. Targets have been found to assign more reasons for bullying to the bully than to the external environment. Jones and Davis (1965) refer to the 'fundamental attribution failure', which suggests people tend to explain their own behaviour by reference to their environment while explaining the behaviour of others by personality. Thus a target of bullying may be blamed for bullying behaviour and their perceptions of bullying dismissed on the grounds of weak personality or over-sensitivity. On the other hand, the over-reliance on self-reports of targets of bullying may equally lead to misinterpretations of events as the target's interpretation may not be the only or entirely valid account.

Intent

Intent to cause offence is generally not included in definitions of bullying and harassment. This is because intent is very difficult to prove and because it is the effect on the target that is of primary importance. Thus the fact that the perpetrator may not have intended to engage in bullying or harassment does not make the act any less serious.

Role of the media and trade unions

Since the early 1990s, increasing media and trade union interest has been important in establishing bullying as a legitimate form of workplace victimisation whereas before unfair working practices were often seen as an integral part of social relations at work. Furthermore, descriptions of types of bullying behaviour such as those given in **TABLE 1** have been of great importance in giving men and women legitimate labels for their experiences.

PSYCHOLOGICAL AND PHYSICAL SIGNS THAT SOMEONE IS BEING BULLIED

There is clear evidence that exposure to systematic and long-lasting bullying behaviour in the workplace causes a range of negative health effects in the targets (Zapf & Einarsen, 2001). A small number of recent studies have consistently shown that social conflict, negative relationships and abusive supervision are related to depression and symptoms of poor mental health.

The UMIST study (Hoel and Cooper, 2000) found higher levels of mental and physical ill health in victims of bullying than other groups in the general population. In a study in Germany, Gaarst et al (2000) found that conflicts and animosities were related to increased reports of depression. In another study of 1,800 individuals in the UK it was found that those who reported they had been bullied were significantly more likely to report higher levels of work–related stress (Smith *et al.*, 2000). However, the same study showed that there was no significant link between those who reported sexual or racial abuse and work stress.

A US general population survey showed that those who reported abusive styles of supervision were significantly more likely to leave their jobs within six months and more likely to experience higher levels of conflict between family and work, lower work commitment and lower job and life satisfaction (Tepper, 2000). The study also showed that reports of abusive supervision were also significantly associated with reports of depression, emotional exhaustion and anxiety. Finally, a study of UK civil servants (Stansfeld *et al.*, 1998) found there was a significant relationship between those reporting highly negative relationships at work and depression, anxiety and emotional exhaustion six months on.

Broadly speaking, the psychological and physical signs that someone is being bullied relate to symptoms of stress. Stress is defined by the Health and Safety Executive (2003) as 'the adverse reaction that people have to excessive pressure and other types of demand placed on them.' Clearly, it is difficult to separate the symptoms of stress caused by bullying and those caused by other life events. However, significant changes in an individual's behaviour at work should always be a cause for concern and investigation. Such changes may include a drop in work performance of a previously competent member of staff, lack of motivation, emotional withdrawal, increased absenteeism and poor time-keeping where there was previously a good attendance record, and hypersensitivity where the individual interprets almost every communication as a threat or criticism. More difficult to identify will be increased addictive behaviours such as smoking and drinking alcohol.

Numerous other symptoms of bullying have been described. The Andrea Adams Trust suggests that those who have been bullied may suffer from the following: disturbed sleep, feeling sick, headaches, palpitations, panic attacks, sweating, shaking, stomach/bowel problems, frequent aches/pains/infections, numbness, trembling, loss of appetite, loss of libido, acute anxiety, loss of confidence, feeling isolated, loss of self-esteem and motivation, depression, anger, and obsessive behaviour. Bully OnLine lists many other symptoms of stress such as reduced immunity to infection leading to various illnesses, panic attacks, poor memory and concentration, tearfulness, mood swings and reactive depression. There are also other physical symptoms such as high blood pressure and chest pains.

Finally it is important to note that bullying and harassment may have extremely serious and possibly life-threatening effects. A number of empirical studies have linked bullying to Post Traumatic Stress Disorder (PTSD) or to PTSD-like symptoms (e.g. Mikkelsen & Einarsen, 2002). PTSD may result in personality change with two predominantly anxiety-related effects – severe depression and serious obsession. In earlier work Leymann (1990, 1992) has claimed that work harassment may account for a number of suicides, although these findings have been seen as controversial.

IDENTIFYING VULNERABLE INDIVIDUALS AND GROUPS

There is no consistent picture of the people most vulnerable to bullying. Clearly an organisation needs to pay particular attention to the minority groups within its workforce, such as people from ethnic minorities, those with disabilities and those with minority religious beliefs or sexual orientation.

However a survey by UNISON (1997) found that, based on 760 responses, those who labelled themselves bullied were not significantly different in terms of gender, position, sector, race and age from the sample as a whole. Most studies conclude there is little difference in the incidence of bullying for both men and women (Hoel, Rayner and Cooper, 1999). One study found that older employees reported more exposure to victimisation than younger employees (Einarsen and Skogstad, 1996). It explained these findings on the basis that as employees grow older they may expect to be treated with more dignity and respect, and so have a lower threshold for what they regard as acceptable treatment.

In contrast, Hoel & Cooper (2000) found that young respondents reported more negative behaviours than older respondents. The two behaviours that stood out were unwanted sexual attention and being given jobs outside their job description. The authors concluded that young and inexperienced workers might be particularly vulnerable to this kind of exploitation. In the same study, respondents of Asian or Afro-Caribbean origin reported particularly high frequencies of personal insults. A survey of workplace bullying among junior doctors (Quine, 2002) found black and Asian doctors were more likely to be bullied than doctors of other origins.

There is evidence that cultural differences play an important part in the occurrence of bullying/harassment among certain groups. For example, one study of women working in male-dominated industrial organisations in the US and Norway found Norwegian women reported less unwanted sexual attention than American women (Einarsen, 2000). It suggested the egalitarian Norwegian culture dictates that men should be less aggressive and dominating than in the US.

The study also points to evidence that individual temperament and personality traits may affect a target's reaction to victimisation. Some personalities may respond to bullying in a more optimistic, flexible way than others. Targets who are at ease in social relationships, who have a positive self-image and who feel they can influence events, may manage better than others when faced with interpersonal conflicts. A final point by Einarsen relates to social support: people who have a strong social network, either in or out of work, are probably less vulnerable to bullying than those who do not.

It is not only the targets of bullying/harassment who may be adversely affected; such behaviour may also have negative effects on observers and witnesses. It has been speculated that those who have witnessed bullying are more likely to leave their organisation on the grounds that they do not wish to be part of an organisation where bullying takes place and where they might be a future target.

IDENTIFYING PROBLEMS

There are a number of information-gathering techniques that can help to identify problems within an organisation.

Risk assessment and risk management

Traditional risk assessment and risk management techniques may be useful in identifying potential problems and preventing them before they occur. The assessment should identify those factors present in the work environment that are known to be associated with bullying and harassment (see **CHAPTER 2**); it should decide who may be harmed by these hazards and what precautions need to be taken to prevent such harm; it should also record the findings and review the assessment at regular intervals.

Staff attitude surveys and questionnaires

Staff attitude surveys can be a helpful way of eliciting information about employee attitudes to how the organisation is managing bullying and harassment and many organisations undertake such surveys on a regular basis. They allow a large amount of data to be collected in a relatively short time and for a range of statistical analyses to be undertaken. Questions can be included about the degree of confidence the individual has in the organisation's ability to identify and tackle bullying/harassment and whether the individual feels the organisation's management processes and culture is supportive. In addition, a survey can also ask for information about incidents of bullying/harassment, either experienced at first hand or observed, which may alert the organisation to problems requiring management intervention.

One of the main disadvantages of questionnaires and attitude surveys in relation to bullying and harassment is that they rely on the self-reports of individuals. In addition the questionnaire format makes it difficult to elicit detailed information about the kind of bullying that may have been experienced. Finally, respondents are generally self-selecting, thus producing a bias in the results.

Focus groups

The technique of interviewing individuals in focus groups is widely used in market research to assist organisations to gain a better understanding of their customers' perceptions and attitudes. But they have also been used to collect information on a wide range of issues including workplace bullying. Focus groups could provide both detailed information about what specific behaviours staff perceive as bullying or harassment and also about the incidence of bullying and harassment in the organisation. However, forums for discussing such sensitive issues need to be well-managed. For example, the facilitator needs to take care that the discussion is not dominated by a few individuals and that confidentiality and ethical issues are adequately addressed.

Exit interviews

In a number of organisations, human resources staff interview some or all staff who have resigned in order to gain a better understanding of why they are leaving. Such interviews may elicit information about bullying and whether it has played a part in the individual's decision to leave. However, while interviews can provide in-depth information, they are time-consuming and the interviewer needs to be skilled in discussing such sensitive topics. In addition, exit interviews could be used by disgruntled employees as a form of revenge or trouble-making and therefore should not be seen as entirely reliable sources of information.

Other steps

In addition to the establishment of an effective anti-bullying/dignity at work policy (see **CHAPTER 6**), there are four other steps that an organisation may consider taking in order to prevent and address bullying and harassment. These are:

1. establish organisational standards of behaviour

2. employee assistance programmes and counselling services

3. mediation

4. review of management styles and attitudes.

Establish organisational standards of behaviour

ACAS (2003) suggests that a statement issued by the organisation to all staff about the standards of behaviour expected makes it easier for individuals to be aware of their responsibilities to others. This information could also be included in other publications such as the staff handbook or a special guidance booklet. It should also be included in training workshops and seminars on bullying and harassment to increase staff awareness of the sort of behaviours that will not be tolerated by the organisation.

Employee assistance programmes (EAPs) and counselling services

EAPs are programmes that provide support to employees in various ways. They usually include counselling services for employees to contact, which can provide confidential support for individuals who are experiencing bullying or harassment at work and may also offer help in resolving the problem, often through informal routes.

Mediation

Many organisations are introducing mediation as a way of preventing conflict between individuals escalating into a formal complaint (see **CHAPTER 6**). However, to be effective, mediation must be entered into voluntarily by all the parties involved at an early stage in the conflict. Once the situation has escalated it could be difficult for victims to participate in mediation and accept any sort of negotiated solution. Mediation may be used to resolve all kinds of conflict in the workplace including bullying, harassment and discrimination. Managers can be given training in mediation skills to provide an in house resource. Alternatively mediators from external providers may be used.

Review of management styles and attitudes

Research has shown that a great deal of bullying is perpetrated by the target's manager or supervisor and therefore abusive styles of management behaviour need to be addressed. Several authors have commented on the lack of attention to negative styles and attitudes in the management/leadership literature (Hoel *et al.*, 1999). Management training tends to concentrate on the positive aspects of being an effective manager or leader and ignore the negative behaviours that need to be reduced or eliminated.

Organisations, therefore, need to look critically at management style within the organisation. Management training should include specific training on bullying and harassment, the types of behaviour that are unacceptable and information about those staff who are likely to be most vulnerable. Organisations should also offer support to managers in managing their own emotions and increasing their self-awareness and sensitivity when dealing with subordinates. In addition, managers should be aware of the importance of creating and maintaining supportive working relationships in order to reduce incidents of bullying and harassment and improve the well-being of staff at work.

As we have seen above, strong management can easily cross the line into bullying behaviour. ACAS stresses that a culture in which employees are consulted and problems are openly discussed is less likely to foster bullying and harassment than one where there is a more authoritarian management style. This view is supported by Hoel and Cooper (2000) who propose that the confrontational and aggressive management style so often favoured by American business schools needs to be challenged and replaced with more co-operative styles based on integrity, ethical behaviour and consideration for the needs of staff.

CONCLUSION

Bullying and harassment are complex social issues and there are no universally agreed definitions or lists of behaviours. There is, however, some convergence on the types of behaviours that may constitute bullying and there is also recognition that a great deal of bullying is undertaken by the target's supervisor/manager and is related to a negative management style. It is probably not possible to eliminate bullying from the workplace entirely, but a crucial first step is for organisations to define and communicate the standards of behaviour they expect both from staff and managers.

REFERENCES AND RESOURCES

Books, journal papers and surveys

Cowie H, Naylor P, Rivers I, Smith P K, Pereira B (2002) 'Measuring workplace bullying' in *Aggression and Violent Behaviour* 7 pp 33–51.

Einarsen S (2000) 'Harassment and Bullying at Work: A Review of the Scandinavian Approach' in *Aggression and Violent Behavior* 5(4) pp 379–401.

Einarsen S and Skogstad A (1996) 'Bullying at work: epidemiological findings in public and private organisations' in *European Journal of Work and Organizational Psychology* 5 pp 185–201.

Gaarst H, Frese M, Molenaar P C M (2000) 'The Temporal Factor of Change in Stressor-Strain Relationships; A Growth Curve Model on a Longitudinal Study in East Germany' in *Journal of Applied Psychology* 85(3) pp 417–438.

Hoel H and Cooper C L (2000) *Destructive conflict and bullying at work*, Manchester School of Management, University of Manchester Institute of Science and Technology (UMIST).

Hoel H, Rayner C, and Cooper C L (1999) 'Workplace Bullying' Chapter 5 of *International Review of Industrial and Organizational Psychology* 14 pp 195–230.

Jones E E and Davis K E (1965) 'From acts to dispositions: The attribution process in person perception' in I L Berkowitz (ed) *Advances in Experimental Social Psychology* 2 New York: Academic Press.

Lewis D (2003) 'Voices in the social construction of bullying at work: exploring multiple realities in further and higher education' in *International Journal of Management and Decision Making* 4(1) pp 65–81.

Leymann H (1990) 'Mobbing and psychological terror at workplaces' in *Violence and Victims* 5 pp 119–126.

Leymann H (1996) 'The content and development of mobbing at work' in *European Journal of Work and Organizational Psychology* 5(2) pp 165–184.

Liefooghe A P D and Olfasson R (1999) 'Scientists and "amateurs": mapping the bullying domain' in *International Journal of Manpower* 20, Issue 1–2.

Mickelson E V and Einarsen S (2002) 'Basic assumptions and symptoms of post-traumatic stress among victims of bullying at work' in *European Journal of Work and Organizational Psychology* 11(1) pp 87–111.

Quine L (2002) 'Workplace bullying in junior doctors: questionnaire survey' in *British Medical Journal* 324 pp 878–879.

Smith A, Johal S, Wadsworth E, Davey Smith G and Peters T (2000) 'The Scale of Occupational Stress: The Bristol Stress and Health and Safety at Work Study' in *Health and Safety Executive*, Contract Research Report 265, HSE Books.

Stansfeld S A, Bosma H, Hemingway H and Marmot M G (1998) 'Psychosocial Work Characteristics and Social Support as Predictors of SF-36 Health Functioning: The Whitehall II Study' in *Psychosomatic Medicine* 60 pp 247–255.

Tepper B (2000) 'Consequences of Abusive Supervision' in *Academy of Management Journal* 43(2) pp 178–190.

UNISON (1997) *Bullying at work*, Unison Bullying Survey Report.

Zapf D and Einarsen S (2001) 'Bullying in the workplace: Recent trends in research and practice – an introduction' in *European Journal of Work and Organizational Psychology* 10(4) pp 369–373.

Website resources

Advisory, Conciliation and Arbitration Service (2003), Bullying and Harassment at Work: A Guide for Managers and Employers
http://www.acas.org.uk/publications/AL04.html *(accessed 23 December 2003)*.

Andrea Adams Trust, (2003), Factsheet on Workplace Bullying
http://www.andreaadamstrust.org/Factsheetpdf.pdf *(accessed 31 December 2003)*.

Bully OnLine (2003), Stress, Injury to Health, Trauma, PTSD
http://www.bullyonline.org/stress/health.htm *(accessed 30 December 2003)*.

Bully OnLine (2003), Those who can do, those who can't bully
http://www.bullyonline.org/workbully/bully.htm *(accessed 31 December 2003)*.

Chartered Institute of Personnel and Development (2002) Bullying at Work, Quick Facts
http://cipd.co.uk/Infosource/EqualityandDiversity/Bullying.asp *(accessed 7 December 2003)*.

Chartered Institute of Personnel and Development (2002) Harassment at Work, Quick Facts
http://cipd.co.uk/Infosource/EqualityandDiversity/Harassment.asp *(accessed 7 December 2003)*.

Health and Safety Executive (2003) Work-related stress
http://www.hse.gov.uk/stress/index.htm *and* *http://www.hse.gov.uk/stress/index.htm* *(accessed 30 December 2003).*

Chapter Five

The Employer's Duty of Care: The Law

Heather Falconer

INTRODUCTION

There are many complex and overlapping legal duties employers must discharge in relation to conflict in the workplace. Whether cheeky office banter and insult-trading, bullying management tactics, or out-and-out assault and battery, conflict-based behaviours and their aftermath create obligations (and therefore potential liabilities) not only towards the victims but also sometimes towards the perpetrators.

HEALTH AND SAFETY DUTIES GENERALLY

The Health and Safety at Work etc. Act 1974 (HSWA) is the core piece of legislation concerning health and safety. Breaches of health and safety obligations by an employer can lead to:

- enforcement action by the Health and Safety Executive (HSE)

- civil claims from employees and others

- employment tribunal claims from employees

- criminal sanction against individual employees, directors and other senior officers, the owners of the business and, if that business is a body corporate, the body corporate itself.

There is a general duty on every employer under the HSWA to ensure, 'so far as is reasonably practicable, the health, safety and welfare at work of all his employees'.

That general duty extends to ensuring, so far as is reasonably practicable, that the place and system of work is safe. This means not only ensuring the physical infrastructure of the workplace is controlled but that employees are not exposed to 'psychosocial' hazards, for example high levels of stress which could cause them harm such as stress-related mental and physical illness.

Deciding what is reasonably practicable involves balancing the risk of injury against the cost and effort of taking measures to eliminate or reduce the risk. If the risk is insignificant compared to the sacrifice, then compliance will not be deemed reasonably practicable. The employer must make its own judgment as to whether or not the safety measures should be implemented.

Employers have general duties under the Management of Health and Safety at Work Regulations 1999 (MHSWR) to carry out a hazard analysis study of the workplace and work activity, to work out what hazards there might be that could cause employees harm. They are then under an obligation to undertake risk assessments to weigh up the likelihood of those hazards causing harm and put in place appropriate measures to guard against such harm being caused if necessary.

If a safety precaution is reasonably practicable it must be taken 'unless in the whole circumstances that would be unreasonable'.

However, there are judicially recognised limits. In Dutton & Clark Ltd v Daly [1985] IRLR 363, EAT, the EAT admitted that the employer cannot guarantee a risk-free environment. The claimant worked in a building society which experienced an armed robbery. She argued that the employer was in breach of duty for failing to protect her better from such dangers. However, the court said the employer had done all that it was reasonably practicable to do to provide for her health and safety.

Employers are also under a duty under the HSWA to ensure, so far as is reasonably practicable, that non-employees are not exposed to health and safety risks. This will include sub-contractors and their employees, visitors to the premises, temporary, agency and casual workers.

The legislation requires employers to take greater care of more vulnerable employees, whether that is because they are pregnant, lacking in experience or maturity, disabled, or suffering from pre-existing mental or physical injury. The MHSWR specifically require employers to take account of the individual's capabilities when assessing risks, particularly in the case of pregnant women and young people.

The legislation also places duties on employees to take reasonable care for the health and safety of him or herself and others (a breach of this particular provision can result in criminal liability); report any serious and imminent danger; and report any matter that he or she reasonably considers to be a shortcoming in the employer's health and safety arrangements.

HEALTH AND SAFETY DUTIES AND STRESS

It is much harder to identify psychosocial hazards – working conditions which may cause individuals to suffer high and potentially harmful levels of stress and anxiety and consequently psychological injury – than physical stress. It is well known that different environments affect different people in different ways – people can cope with varying levels of pressure and many are not even aware themselves whether and how pressures might be affecting them, never mind able to make the employer aware. It may also be hard to distinguish between stress caused mainly by work, for which an employer is liable, and stress caused mainly by other things, for which it is not. Therefore fitting psychosocial hazards into the framework of health and safety duties – identifying hazards, assessing if and how these might cause harm, and putting measures in place to prevent that harm where reasonably practicable – is still at an experimental stage. Some say it simply cannot be done.

Nevertheless, the HSE has made it clear that work-related stress can be a hazard to health and that employers must discharge their duties under the health and safety legislation in relation to stress in the same way as they do for other potential hazards in the workplace. To make it easier for employers, it provides guidance on its website (**http://www.hse.gov.uk**) on what kind of stress-related hazards employers should look for, how they can gather information on whether employees are affected, and how they can take steps to try to avoid harm.

The HSE is also in the midst of a project to develop management standards on stress, which employers and enforcement agencies will eventually be able to use to decide if workplaces are organised in such a way that workers are at risk from stress. At present, there are no firm plans to make these management standards mandatory – they are stated as being for 'guidance only' – but the HSE has said that in the future, following extensive testing and feedback from employers, it may take enforcement action under the health and safety legislation against employers who do not comply with the standards.

The HSE stress management standards are categorised under seven headings. One of these is 'Relationships'. In this category, employers must show that at least 65 per cent of employees indicate that they are not subjected to unacceptable behaviours (e.g. bullying) at work; and that systems are in place locally to respond to any individual concerns.

The HSE states that in order to meet the standard, organisations should aim for a 'state to be achieved' where:

- the organisation has, in place, agreed procedures to effectively prevent or quickly resolve conflict at work

- these procedures are agreed with employees and their representatives and enable employees to confidentially report any concerns they might have

- the organisation has a policy for dealing with unacceptable behaviour at work. This has been agreed with employees and their representatives

- the policy for dealing with unacceptable behaviour at work has been widely communicated in the organisation

- consideration is given to the way teams are organised to ensure they are cohesive, have a sound structure, clear leadership and objectives

- employees are encouraged to talk to their line manager, employee representative, or external provider about any behaviours that are causing them concern at work

- individuals in teams are encouraged to be open and honest with each other and are aware of the penalties associated with unacceptable behaviour.

NEGLIGENCE

As well as their duties under the health and safety legislation, employers have a duty under negligence law to take reasonable care of the health, safety and welfare of their employees. This is not an absolute duty, but if an employee falls ill as a result of the employer's negligence, the organisation could be liable. The employee would have to show that it was the employer's acts or failure to act that caused them to be harmed, and that any reasonable employer should have foreseen harm of the type suffered and taken steps to prevent it.

Damages are awarded on the principle that they should put the individual in the position they would have been in had the negligence not occurred. There will be compensation for loss of earnings as a result of injury with an additional amount for pain and suffering. In serious cases, damages can amount to hundreds of thousands of pounds.

Employers will be liable if they are aware or should be aware of conflict in the workplace that is having a serious effect on their workers and they do nothing about it. This was established by the House of Lords in the case of Waters v Commissioner of the Metropolis [1997]. A female police officer complained internally that she had been raped by a fellow officer while off duty at the police residences. She alleged her employer failed to deal with the complaint and 'caused and/or permitted officers to maliciously criticise, harm, victimise, threaten, assault and otherwise oppress her' in a campaign of victimisation.

The House of Lords agreed that this amounted to negligence, although it stressed that it was not every case of conflict between employees that would render the employer liable, and that an employee 'may have to accept some degree of unpleasantness from fellow workers'.

STRESS AND PERSONAL INJURY

It is this area of the law that has spawned a spate of personal injury claims for stress-related illness in recent years. These started in 1995 with the Walker v Northumberland County Council [1995] IRLR 35 case, where the claimant won £500,000 after suffering a second nervous breakdown due to work pressures. He successfully argued that the employer should reasonably have foreseen the danger to his ill health mainly because he had already suffered one nervous breakdown and the council did not take action to relieve his workload.

In 2002, the Court of Appeal took the opportunity, in four related cases on stress collectively known as Sutherland v Hatton [2002] EWCA Civ 76, to clarify the rules on employer liability. 'Without a real risk of injury that the employer ought reasonably to have foreseen and ought properly to have averted, there can be no liability,' the ruling said.

In its judgment, the Court of Appeal set out the following points that need to be applied in deciding when an employer should be liable for illness arising from work-related stress:

- There are no special control mechanisms applying to claims for psychiatric illness or injury arising from the stress of doing the work the employee is required to do. The ordinary principles of employer's liability apply.

- The threshold question is whether this kind of harm to this particular employee was reasonably foreseeable. This has two components: (a) an injury to health which (b) is attributable to stress at work.

- Foreseeability depends on what the employer knows (or ought reasonably to know) about the individual employee. Because of the nature of mental disorder, it is harder to foresee than physical injury, but may be easier to foresee in a known individual than in the population at large.

- There are no occupations which should be regarded as intrinsically dangerous to mental health.

- Factors likely to be relevant in answering the threshold question include:

  — The nature of the work done by the employee. For example, are there signs that others doing this job are suffering harmful levels of stress? Is there an abnormal level of sickness or absenteeism in the same job or the same department?

  — Signs from the employee of impending harm to health. Has he a particular problem or vulnerability? Has he already suffered from illness attributable to stress at work? Have there recently been frequent or prolonged absences which are uncharacteristic of him? Is there reason to think that these are attributable to stress at work, for example because of complaints or warnings from him or others?

- The employer is generally entitled to take what he is told by his employee at face value, unless he has good reason to think to the contrary.

- The indications of impending harm to health arising from stress at work must be plain enough for any reasonable employer to realise that he should do something about it.

- The employer is only in breach of duty if he has failed to take the steps which are reasonable in the circumstances.

- The size and scope of the employer's operation, its resources and the demands it faces are relevant in deciding what is reasonable; these include the interests of other employees.

- An employer can only reasonably be expected to take steps which are likely to do some good.

- An employer who offers a confidential advice service, with referral to appropriate counselling or treatment services, is unlikely to be found in breach of duty.

- If the only reasonable and effective step would have been to dismiss or demote the employee, the employer will not be in breach of duty in allowing a willing employee to continue in the job.

- In all cases, therefore, it is necessary to identify the steps which the employer both could and should have taken before finding him in breach of his duty of care.

DISCRIMINATION

An employer can be liable for the harassment of an employee by other employees and sometimes by third parties on the grounds of sex, race, disability, religion and sexual orientation – and in the future, on the grounds of age too.

For the first time in British law, the Employment Equality Regulations 2003 on sexual orientation and religious belief introduced a statutory definition of harassment as 'unwanted conduct which takes place with the purpose or effect of violating the dignity of a person and of creating an intimidating, hostile, degrading, humiliating or offensive environment'.

Before this, however, the courts had long recognised that harassment was a form of direct discrimination under the Sex Discrimination Act 1975 (SDA), the Race Relations Act 1976 (RRA) and the disability Discrimination Act 1995 (DDA). They relied on the European Commission's code of practice on the Protection of the Dignity of Women and Men at Work when hearing sexual harassment cases. This definition is also very wide – it defines harassment as unwanted conduct of a sexual nature, or other conduct based on sex affecting the dignity of women and men at work. This can include unwelcome physical, verbal or even non-verbal behaviour.

The code states that such conduct is unacceptable where it is unwanted, unreasonable and offensive to the recipient; where the individual's response to the treatment affects their employment; or where it creates an intimidating, hostile or humiliating work environment for the recipient.

It does not matter if the alleged perpetrator had no intention of causing offence – perhaps he or she was merely partaking in 'harmless' banter or sending an offensive email which someone else saw by accident. Whether the employer is liable for those acts depends on how the claimant actually reacted and felt, rather than the intention of the harasser.

In most cases, harassment will be a course or pattern of behaviour which becomes harassment once the recipient makes it clear she or he finds it unwelcome and the perpetrator persists. But a single incident may be harassment if it is sufficiently serious or offensive, such as sexually or racially motivated assault or an extremely offensive remark.

For the employer to be liable for the actions of employees, the harasser must have been acting 'in the course of employment'. However, an employer does not have to have authorised the conduct, or even have any knowledge of it, to be liable.

In the case of Jones v Tower Boot Company (1997 CA), Jones was the victim of constant racial harassment by co-workers. His arm was burnt with a hot screwdriver, metal bolts were thrown at him and he was called names such as 'chimp', 'monkey' and 'baboon'. The employer argued these acts were outside the course of employment as it had not authorised them and did not know they were going on. This was rejected by the Court of Appeal: it said the words 'in the course of employment' should be interpreted in the sense in which they are employed in everyday speech, otherwise the worst harassment cases would not be covered by the legislation.

The conduct does not need to be on the employer's premises or even within working hours for liability to arise. In one case an employer was found liable for harassment taking place at a leaving party after work when all those involved were off duty. However, in another, the employer was held not to be liable for sexual advances made by an employee at a colleague's home.

In the case of Sidhu v Aerospace Composite Technology Ltd [2002] IRLR 602, a fight broke out between employees on a family day out at a theme park after a Sikh employee was subjected to racist remarks. In these circumstances, the Court of Appeal said the tribunal was not wrong to rule there was no vicarious liability as the harassment was perpetrated outside the workplace, in the employee's free time, and the majority of those present were family and friends rather than employees, and so it was not done in the course of employment. However, the court said another tribunal could have been justified in finding that it was in the course of employment.

Employers should therefore be aware that while it is unlikely liability will arise where harassment takes place at a victim's home or, say, in the pub after work, it may arise if the victim is at a social event connected with work and attends in his or her capacity as an employee.

THE REASONABLE STEPS DEFENCE

Section 41(3) of the SDA and section 32(3) of the RRA provide that an employer will not be liable for the discrimination if it can prove it took such steps as were reasonably practicable to prevent it taking place.

The tribunals have developed this defence to make it fairly onerous on the employer. While having equal opportunities and harassment policies and procedures in place will be important, it is also important to ensure that staff are aware of and trained in the procedures.

In the case of Canniffe v East Riding of Yorkshire Council (EOR 93), the EAT said even though the council had harassment, grievance and disciplinary policies in place, this was not necessarily enough to discharge their duties. The tribunal should still have asked what further steps the employer could have taken, and then asked whether it would have been reasonably practicable to take them.

NEW FORMS OF DISCRIMINATION

The EU Employment Framework Directive provides it is unlawful to discriminate on the grounds of religious belief, sexual orientation or age. This has resulted in the UK's Employment Equality (Sexual Orientation) Regulations 2003 (SOR), which came into force on 1 December 2003. The Employment Equality (Religion or Belief) Regulations 2003 (RBR) came into force the following day. These Regulations protect employees and some other workers against harassment and victimisation on the grounds of sexual orientation, religion or belief. Discrimination on the grounds of age is due to be outlawed in 2006.

Under the SOR it is unlawful to discriminate against, harass or victimise a person on the basis of their sexual orientation towards partners of the:

- same sex

- opposite sex or

- both sexes.

Under the RBR, 'religion or belief' is defined as any religion, religious belief or similar philosophical belief. The Regulations do not provide a list but say that a philosophical or political belief is not covered unless that belief is 'similar to' a religious belief. It will be up to the tribunals to decide which belief systems are covered. Factors that may be taken into consideration include whether there is any collective worship, a clear belief system, or a profound belief reflecting a way of life or view of the world.

'Manifestations' of a religion or belief are also protected. Harassment and discrimination based on *perceived* sexual orientation, religion or belief, even if that perception is wrong, is covered by the Regulations, as is direct discrimination against a person based on the sexual orientation, religion or belief of someone else such as friends or family.

As with older discrimination law, employers are liable for acts of discrimination carried out by their employees in the course of their employment, unless they can show that they took such steps as were reasonably practicable to prevent them.

Whether someone has been harassed is considered on the basis of whether, in all the circumstances, including in particular the perception of the complainant, it should reasonably be considered as having that effect. This means over-sensitive employees who take offence unreasonably are probably not protected.

Similarly, victimisation is defined as less favourable treatment because the complainant brought proceedings under the Regulations; gave evidence/information in connection with such proceedings; did anything under/by reference to the Regulations or alleged that anyone had committed an act which (whether or not the allegation said so) would amount to a contravention of the Regulations or because the discriminator knows the complainant intends to do any of those things or suspects that the complainant has done/intends to do any of them. There is no victimisation if the allegation, evidence or information was false and not made or given in good faith.

BREACH OF CONTRACT

As well as their statutory and common law duties, employers have a duty under the employment contract not to breach the implied term of mutual trust and confidence. This means employers and those in whom they entrust the operation of the employment relationship, such as managers, must not treat an employee in a way that is calculated or likely to destroy or seriously damage the relationship, which is one based on confidence and trust.

This implied term has been invoked more and more since the late 1970s by employees in a wide range of conflict situations. One of the earliest cases, Courtaulds Northern Textiles Ltd v Andrew [1979] IRLR 84, was brought by an employee who had worked as an overseer for the textile company for 18 years. During the course of an argument with one of his managers, the manager said to him: 'You can't do the bloody job anyway'. Andrew immediately resigned and claimed constructive dismissal, arguing he was justified in doing so because of the nature of the comment and the fact there was no truth in it. The EAT upheld his claim.

Since then the implied term of mutual trust and confidence has been used successfully to claim compensation for constructive dismissal following a whole range of ill-judged, overly critical, abusive or bullying remarks and treatment, such as when a supermarket bakery manager was harshly criticised and threatened with the sack by her boss in earshot of customers, or when a manager said of his secretary in her presence: 'She's an intolerable bitch on a Monday morning'.

The key in such cases is whether the behaviour or comments are so serious that they entitle the employee to walk out immediately, claiming the employer has breached the terms of the contract to such an extent that they no longer bind the parties together. This is known in legal terms as a 'repudiatory breach'. Whether there has been such a breach is for tribunals to decide on the facts of the case. In the case of Moores v Bude Stratton Town Council [2001] ICR 271, the tribunal indicated some of the factors that will be taken into account. In this case the employer was held liable for the constructive dismissal of an employee after a councillor said of him: 'I shouldn't talk to that lying toe-rag – he's not worth it'.

The tribunal said the material considerations were whether the comments or treatment came from someone in the organisation who could be deemed to have the employer's authority; whether the employer dealt with the matter swiftly and offered an immediate retraction or apology; whether the employee was overly sensitive or inflexible in insisting the contract was effectively at an end or refusing to accept the employer's apology; whether the incident could have been foreseen by the employer and therefore averted; and whether the employee's behaviour contributed to or was equally as reprehensible as that of the employer.

Whether the behaviour is deemed to be authorised by the employer, and therefore to carry the threat of liability, depends partly on the seniority of the perpetrator. But even junior managers could trigger liability if they do not treat other employees in a respectful way. It is therefore the employer's duty to ensure that all those in whom they have entrusted the management of the employment relationship under the terms of the contract act out those responsibilities appropriately, through proper recruitment, written policies, training and development.

Having, using and training employees in grievance and disciplinary procedures is important in ensuring that cases are dealt with in such a way that the employment relationship can be protected or salvaged.

DISMISSAL

Employers have a duty under the Employment Rights Act 1996 (ERA) not to dismiss employees unfairly. Dismissal must be for a reason that falls within one of the categories set out in section 98(2) of the ERA: capability or qualifications; conduct; redundancy; statutory requirements; or 'some other substantial reason' justifying dismissal.

It is up to the employer to show the reason for dismissal and that it is a potentially fair reason. The tribunal will then decide if the employer acted fairly in dismissing for that reason, though there is no burden of proof on the employer to show this. The test the tribunal will apply is whether dismissal was a reasonable action open to the employer in the circumstances. This implies that there are a whole range of possible ways an employer can react to, say an instance of misconduct, from the most lenient, such as a verbal warning, to the most severe – summary dismissal – all of which may be broadly reasonable. As long as the action taken is within this range, and not irrational or perverse, the tribunal will find it fair. The test does not allow tribunal panels to decide what they would have done in the circumstances – only whether dismissal falls within the range of reasonable responses.

Conduct dismissals

Many dismissals following cases of conflict between employees will fall into the conduct category. Dismissals for conduct need to be undertaken very carefully, as they will be considered according to how thoroughly the incidents were investigated; the reasonableness of the decision to dismiss; and the fairness of the procedure for discipline and dismissal.

In conduct cases, the employer must show that the decision to dismiss was taken based on an honest belief of misconduct based on reasonable grounds, and that this was the result of a reasonable investigation in all the circumstances.

A common problem that arises in cases involving conflict between employees is whether it is fair to discipline those involved in different ways. The tribunals have held that this is possible as long as the decision to do so is a reasonable one in light of all the facts.

This issue was addressed in the case of UK Coal Mining Limited v Raby [2003] All ER (D) 324, in which two employees got into a fight. The man claiming unfair dismissal started the fight by lightly tapping his colleague with his helmet after he was verbally provoked. He had a written warning on his disciplinary record from several years earlier, which should have been wiped after 12 months in line with the ACAS code of practice to which the organisation normally adhered. He was dismissed because of his record and the fact he started the fight, while his colleague was not.

The tribunal decided that the applicant was justified in claiming this was unfair: it was not reasonable to base the decision on who struck the first blow given that it was not especially violent and that it had been provoked verbally. In addition, the applicant's previous warning should not have been on his record and therefore should not have influenced the decision. This case highlights not only the importance of balancing fairness with individual circumstances, but also the importance of keeping disciplinary records up to date.

Problems can also arise where an employee is dismissed for a gross misconduct offence such as an assault, but claims this is unfair because others committing similar offences in the past have escaped dismissal. In cases such as Procter v British Gypsum Ltd [1991] IRLR 7, the tribunals have stressed that while there is a need for basic consistency, employers must have the ability to consider each case on its own facts.

What if employees get into a group fight, and the employer finds it impossible, despite a thorough investigation, to decide who was responsible for starting or causing it? Is it potentially fair to dismiss all those involved? The precedents suggest that this will be possible if the disciplinary offences of all those in the group justify dismissal; and that after a reasonable investigation the employer decides any one of the group was individually capable of starting the fight but it was not possible to identify which did.

Disciplinary procedures

Following a fair procedure is particularly important in defending unfair dismissal cases involving misconduct, even gross misconduct which might justify summary dismissal (without notice). Generally, unless the employer follows a disciplinary procedure appropriate to the organisation's size and resources, the dismissal will be held unfair.

The tribunals will first look at whether an organisation has followed its own stated disciplinary rules. If it has not, it is unlikely to defend the unfair dismissal claim successfully. Beyond that, the benchmark for tribunals is currently the ACAS code of practice on disciplinary and grievance procedures which provides, for example, for hearings and a right of appeal prior to disciplinary sanctions.

However, the Employment Act 2002 will radically change and simplify the way in which the fairness of dismissals is judged. It provides for new statutory basic disciplinary and grievance procedures, which are due to come into effect in 2004. These will be incorporated into all employees' terms and conditions of employment from day one, so failure to follow them will constitute breach of contract as well as probably unfair dismissal. This will not only mean potentially more compensation, but also that the employer will not be able to rely on other terms of the contract such as post-employment restrictions.

However, provided that employers follow the basic statutory procedures, and the dismissal is found to be for a fair reason and within the range of reasonable responses, the claim should fail. The ACAS code will become more a manual of best practice.

The basic disciplinary procedure consists of three stages:

1. A statement of grounds for action and an invitation to a meeting. The employer must set out in writing to the employee the alleged conduct that has led to the disciplinary action.

2. The meeting, which must take place before any disciplinary action is taken, and the employer must notify the employee of its decision after the meeting.

3. The employee must inform the employer if he or she wishes to appeal. If so, there must be an appeal meeting.

There is a modified procedure for extreme cases of gross misconduct, which omits the need for a meeting prior to dismissal. This will be appropriate only in exceptional circumstances, such as for cases of extreme violence or where a crime is committed, necessitating urgent action.

It will be mandatory for all employers to follow the statutory procedures and failure to do so will render the dismissal automatically unfair. However, it will still be possible to argue that an employee has contributed to his or her dismissal and the tribunal may reduce the compensatory award by between 10 and 50 per cent to reflect this.

GRIEVANCE PROCEDURES

There is a similar three-stage process in The Employment Act 2002 for a basic grievance procedure, which employers and employees are also under an obligation to use. If an employee has a grievance, he or she must send a statement of grievance to the employer and wait 28 days for a response before making a tribunal complaint. The employer must arrange a meeting, and there is provision for an appeal.

Again there is a modified procedure for when the aggrieved individual has left the company. In this case, the employer can respond in writing to the written grievance statement.

If the employee refuses to follow the appropriate statutory procedure, the employment tribunal will not hear the complaint. Tribunal awards will be able to take into account any failure by either the employer or employee to adhere to the procedures, by increasing or reducing the compensation by between 10 and 50 per cent.

WHISTLE-BLOWING

Employees have protection under a number of statutes from victimisation and other detriment as a result of reporting breaches of various laws in the workplace by either employers or other employees.

For example, the Trade Union Reform and Employment Rights Act 1993 protects employees from victimisation for blowing the whistle on breaches of health and safety law, while the Trade Union and Labour Relations (Consolidation) Act 1992 protects employees from victimisation on the grounds of trade union membership or non-membership.

The Public Interest Disclosure Act 1999 (PIDA) introduced much wider protection for whistle-blowers. It renders automatically unfair any dismissal of an employee because they have made a 'protected disclosure'. This includes any disclosure of information which in the reasonable belief of the discloser 'tends to show', for example, a failure to comply with a legal requirement, that a criminal offence has been committed, or that there is danger to health and safety or the environment.

The Act encourages internal disclosures, but provides that serious disclosures to agencies outside the organisation such as the police or relevant authorities may be justified in certain circumstances, such as if the discloser fears internal disclosure will result in victimisation.

There are two important differences between protection under the PIDA and ordinary unfair dismissal protection: first, the PIDA protection does not require any qualifying service; and second, there is no cap on compensation.

The Act has been invoked in a number of cases involving conflict between employees. In A v X (2001), for example, aggravated damages were awarded following an attempt to keep a disclosure of indecent assault secret. Mr A reported complaints by two employees of sexual assaults, after which he and the two victims were threatened with dismissal and slander actions if they mentioned the incidents to anyone. When an employee asked Mr A what was happening to the alleged assailant, Mr A said he might not be coming back. The employers viewed this as a breach of confidence and disciplined Mr A with a written warning. He then went off sick with stress and later resigned. Mr A was awarded £140,000, of which £5,000 was aggravated damages because the employer's behaviour was 'totally inappropriate'.

However, in Fincham v HM Prison Service (2001), it was held that a complaint about spiteful colleagues was not a protected disclosure under the PIDA even though the case revealed a 'hotbed of malice and petty spitefulness'. The grounds were that the employer had breached a legal requirement not to breach the implied term of mutual trust and confidence. The tribunal stated:

> 'Almost every day in almost every workplace employees complain to managers of their treatment by other employees, often with good reason ... The legal requirement on the part of the employer not to breach trust and confidence between employer and employee is not broken by an employer every time an employee behaves badly to another'.

Chapter Six
Establishing Effective Policies

Heather Falconer

INTRODUCTION

HR practitioners spend a good proportion of their working lives working on one type of policy or another. The more traditional sort, with titles such as equal opportunities, sexual harassment, and diversity, are now being added to in progressive companies by initiatives on bullying, violence, whistle-blowing, alcohol and drugs, work-life balance and more.

Recently, some employers have chosen to take a more all-encompassing approach to the problem of dysfunctional conflict such as bullying and harassment by introducing 'dignity at work' policies. These can cover a whole range of conflict issues such as discrimination, harassment, bullying, victimisation, violence. They are designed not only to condemn negative behaviours but also to reinforce the organisation's commitment to positive values such as dignity, respect, courtesy and fairness. They are often couched in terms of the rights and responsibilities of everyone in the workplace.

The impetus for many such policies has been the perceived threat of tribunal claims and the growing likelihood of an employer being held vicariously liable for the illegal acts of its employees: organisations have long been advised that having a clear policy on issues such as harassment and discrimination will reduce the possibility of having to foot the bill.

But this is not all. The past few years has seen a growth in understanding of how fair and ethical employment policies affect employee commitment, loyalty, motivation and retention. The government's Workplace Employee Relations Survey, for example, has found that progressive employment practices result in higher productivity and morale among workers. The growing problems of stress-related illness and absenteeism have also forced some employers to confront the conflict issues causing staff to suffer sustained high levels of anxiety.

Long-term skills shortages have also encouraged employers carefully to examine their images and recruitment branding. Well-communicated ethical policies have proven to be an important way of sending a message to the wider world about the organisation's values, and how these align with prevailing public opinion on social issues. Employers that do this effectively claim to have gained a competitive advantage in a tight labour market, as well as added kudos among consumers, according to a number of studies.

But dignity at work policies will be next to worthless if they are devised by HR practitioners with little input from disinterested senior management – in an attempt, perhaps, to keep up with best practice or even defend against possible tribunal claims – and then left to gather dust on a shelf. No matter how many reams of A4 they consume, they will be a waste of everyone's time and money if staff are not aware of them, nor intimate with their contents and equipped to follow them, in both letter and spirit, in their everyday working lives.

The tribunals have made clear time and again in discrimination cases that employers will only be able to use the 'reasonable steps' defence successfully in relation to harassment (see **PAGE 89**) if their staff are aware of and trained in the policies being brandished as evidence. Banging a beautifully bound booklet down on the tribunal table will do nothing to get the employer off the hook.

But dignity at work policies have a much wider use than merely as a first line of defence in legal claims: they can play a vital role in spear-heading culture change. The key is to ensure that a policy is not introduced into a vacuum: it must have the clear and visible backing of both senior and middle management if it is to have a real effect.

Senior management must 'walk the talk': for instance, if they introduce an anti-bullying policy while continuing to practice and endorse a brand of 'strong' or 'macho' management, the policy will be at best ignored, at worst ridiculed.

As with any culture change initiative, the policy must have the approval and support of line managers, who will be the arbiters of how effectively conflict situations are dealt with. The tone and manner in which they treat and speak to individuals, as well as the procedures they follow, will make or break employees' faith in a policy to foster a healthy, functional workplace culture.

Clearly, this has significant and potentially costly implications: devising and successfully implementing a policy is likely to tie up valuable HR resources, depending on the environment into which it is being introduced. It is not a process to be undertaken lightly.

DEFINING NEEDS AND OBJECTIVES

It is commonly accepted that the more staff are consulted on and involved in devising a policy, the more likely it is to achieve the 'buy-in' necessary to its effectiveness.

How this happens depends on the particular resources and needs of the organisation. For those seeking to use a policy as a force for real cultural change within the organisation, involving a wide cross-section of employee representatives might be an opportunity to demonstrate and nurture commitment to that process. For those wishing merely to formalise what already takes place on an informal and ad-hoc basis, the initial investment may not need to be as high.

Consideration should be given to the setting up of a joint management/employee/trade union working party to guide the policy-making process. This could be done through existing mechanisms for information and consultation or through a specially elected or appointed group.

In order to define the objectives of the policy and monitor its effectiveness, it may be necessary to garner the opinions and attitudes of a wide cross-section of staff, through staff opinion surveys, focus groups or team feedback sessions. This will be of particular importance where the policy is being introduced amid suspicions of widespread dysfunctional behaviour within the organisation – a culture of conflict. In such a situation, gaining knowledge about the attitudes and beliefs of staff and measuring improvement on a regular basis will be a vital tool.

When London Underground introduced its award-winning Ending Harassment programme in 2002, it instigated a wide-ranging consultation exercise which consisted mainly of focus groups of frontline staff, managers and union representatives. These revealed a 'vicious circle of harassment' within the company, a belief that it was hard for victims to complain and a belief that managers were not equipped to deal with the problems. The organisational culture was seen from the inside as one that tolerated sexist and racist behaviour.

Having ascertained these views, the company ran a series of think-tanks involving mixed groups of employees and union representatives, to tackle each of the problems highlighted by staff.

This resulted in the five key strategic objectives for the policy:

1. to establish in partnership with trade unions an effective procedure for dealing with harassment

---

2. to provide independent support for victims

3. to increase the expertise of those dealing with individual cases

4. to establish an effective monitoring system and success indicators

5. to change the organisational culture to one that did not tolerate harassment.

The long-term goal of the policy was to achieve by 2006 a culture:

- free from harassment

- intolerant of prejudice

- where everyone treats each other with respect

- that values diversity.

Source: Equal Opportunities Review, IRS

CONTENT

Policies range from documents that are little more than mission statements to those that set out detailed codes of practice and procedures. Too much detail might be counterproductive if it discourages employees from reading and understanding fully the implications of the policy. It might, therefore, be sensible to combine a fairly succinct and powerful policy statement with referrals to further information in the form of codes of practice or guidelines, perhaps aimed at particular groups.

A policy on dignity at work should contain some or all of the following:

- Explain every worker's right to dignity at work and state that breaches of the right will not be tolerated. This immediately establishes the policy as a positive one that involves everyone in the workplace.

- Acknowledge that this is an issue of importance to the organisation as a whole, and that the policy has the commitment of senior management – this will need to be demonstrated through actions and behaviour.

- Make clear to whom the policy applies, for example, employees, temporary workers and contractors, those working both on and off the premises, visitors to the organisation.

- Set out briefly the responsibilities of various stakeholders of the policy, for example, the CEO and board, head of personnel, senior managers, trade union representatives, employees.

- Set out a brief statement of the standards of behaviour expected and the rights and responsibilities of employees. For example, 'to treat all colleagues and customers with dignity, respect, fairness and courtesy and not to discriminate on the basis of race, religion, gender, sexual orientation, disability, age, or on any other basis'.

- Give definitions and examples of unacceptable behaviour such as bullying, harassment, discrimination and victimisation. You may need separate chapters going into each of these in turn as there are important differences between, say, bullying – which is usually purely psychological, centred on performance issues, often hidden from those around and frequently not recognised as bullying by the victim – and harassment – which is usually motivated by personal qualities (e.g. gender, race), often more open and often with a physical element. Point out that unacceptable behaviour may be verbal (e.g., banter, offensive remarks, swearing), non-verbal (e.g. email, grafitti, offensive gestures) or physical (e.g. inappropriate contact, assault), and that it includes creating or contributing to an unpleasant or unacceptable working environment, whether or not it is directed at any one in particular.

Reigate and Banstead Borough Council's Dignity at Work policy, introduced in 1998, attempts to define acts which contravene the policy as any behaviour which is 'unwanted, unwelcomed and unreciprocated' by the recipient. This encompasses any behaviour that might unreasonably threaten a person's job security or promotion prospects or create an intimidating working environment for an employee or volunteer.

The policy states that a person's dignity at work will be regarded as having been violated if the recipient suffers harassment or bullying or any act, omission, or conduct which causes him or her to be alarmed or distressed, including, but not limited to:

- behaviour on more than one occasion which is offensive, abusive, malicious, insulting or intimidating

- unjustified criticism on more than one occasion

- punishment imposed without reasonable justification

- changes in duties or responsibilities to the detriment of the employee without reasonable justification.

Source: IRS Management Review

- State a commitment to following the company's disciplinary procedure for infringements of the policy, including timescales for action, and refer employees to where that procedure is set out. State examples of behaviour that may constitute gross misconduct giving grounds for immediate dismissal.

- State and ask employees for a commitment to the procedure or procedures (e.g. formal and informal) for reporting grievances and either explain these or refer employees to another easily accessible place where they are set out.

- State a commitment to prompt, thorough, objective and confidential investigation with adequate representation for both complainants and alleged perpetrators.

- State that allegations of breaches of the policy will have to be dealt with in the appropriate way, even if this means going against the victim's wishes, in order to discharge the employer's duty of care towards the workforce as a whole.

- Make available support and advice for both complainants and alleged perpetrators – either by designating independent counsellors within the organisation, or by using an employee assistance programme or specialist counselling organisation – and disseminate contact details.

- Make clear that those found to be making frivolous or malicious allegations will be subject to disciplinary action.

- State how and by whom the policy is to be monitored and reviewed and give ways for employees to offer their views and suggestions for improvement.

Ford of Britain began work on its new Dignity at Work policy in 2001 in collaboration with trade union equality officers. The policy offered employees a range of formal and informal options for dealing with problems, such as talking to their own line manager, or another one if their own is the cause of the problem, a union representative, a member of the HR team, a local diversity council member of the occupational health department. Employee harassment helplines were made available throughout the company for confidential advice and telephone numbers displayed on all local notice boards.

Ford developed three comprehensive guides for employees, managers and investigators, explaining the reasons for introducing the policy, examples of unacceptable behaviour, explaining the law, the procedures for making a complaint and the responsibilities of the respective groups.

About 10,000 Ford managers received a pack of the three guides at their homes along with a letter from the chairman of the company. Plant managers wrote to all employees introducing the policy and asking for their commitment. The information was then cascaded through the organisation via management briefings. Other communications techniques included a poster campaign and publication of material on the Ford of Europe diversity website and company HR intranet. There were also articles in Ford's diversity publication with articles by the president of Ford of Europe and the chair of Ford Financial of Europe.

Source: Equal Opportunities Review

COMMUNICATING THE POLICY

In the first instance, the introduction of a new policy will involve disseminating a copy of the relevant documents to employees along with a letter explaining the policy's importance.

There are numerous considerations here. First, do all employees need to see the full documentation – for example, the policy statement plus accompanying guidance or codes of practice? Or do they need a succinct booklet explaining the essential facts and explaining where to find out more?

Line managers, on the other hand, will merit special recognition of the extra work and skills the policy will entail for them. Are managers likely to be sceptical to begin with? Will they see this as just another burden, a bolt-on to their 'proper' job of meeting targets, deadlines and budgets? If so, they may need a clear explanation of the business case for the policy and a statement of commitment from the top of the organisation, along with an assurance that they will receive the support and training necessary to implement the policy effectively. They may also need more detailed guidance on, for instance, specific examples of unacceptable behaviour, how to spot and deal with conflicts at an early stage before it reaches the stage of a formal complaint, and how to invoke and operate the disciplinary and grievance procedures.

Do customers need their own leaflet, too, explaining the policy, how they can benefit from it and their own obligations towards your staff? Should job applicants receive a summary of the policy too? And what about employees newly promoted to manager? There should be mechanisms in place to ensure they, too, receive all the information relevant to their new role.

How should the documents be sent to employees? Via email? By internal mail? With pay packets? By post to the employee's home? Much depends on the resources available but also on the importance the organisation wishes to attach to the policy. Sending it by post gives out the message that this is something that merits special, undivided attention, and that it is of real personal significance to each individual. An email, on the other hand, risks being lost among the many messages, important, trivial and junk, arriving in inboxes every day.

Careful thought needs to be given to whose name should be at the bottom of the letter. The CEO's signature will obviously give a very real impression that the policy is supported by top management. Who is to have 'ownership' of the policy? If it is local managers, then they may be the ones to communicate initially with their staff and ask for their commitment.

This initial launch may need to be backed up by face-to-face briefings, giving employees the chance to ask questions and clarify their roles if necessary. Core awareness-raising should generally start with senior management briefing managers, either through existing regular meetings or at special extra briefings, and this will then be cascaded down through the organisation. Other techniques such as travelling 'road-shows', staffed by representatives from, say, senior management, HR, and any trade unions involved, and promotional videos and websites can also be used to reinforce the process.

Culture change takes time, and for a dignity at work policy to be effective, staff need to be regularly reminded of it and of the organisation's commitment to it. This could be done through a periodical newsletter – either on paper or via a dedicated site on the company intranet or online HR resource. These can reinforce the importance of the policy by:

- explaining the company's rationale and aims in introducing the policy

- sharing information on the positive effects of the policy

- providing illustrations of other organisations who have already implemented successful policies

- featuring interviews with senior managers on their attitudes to dignity at work and how the policy is informing their own work

- carrying anonymous case studies of problems which have been successfully resolved

- encouraging feedback from managers and staff on how the policy is working and how it might be improved and disseminating this where appropriate

- reiterating the procedures involved in making and investigating complaints and giving out relevant contact details such as telephone helplines or confidential counselling.

Staff and even customer notice-boards are another important source of information – an eye-catching, hard-hitting poster campaign can do much to remind employees and/or customers of their responsibilities and rights under a dignity at work policy and can remind those thinking of raising a complaint of the relevant contact numbers.

TRAINING

Training staff and managers in the policy is perhaps the most crucial element in ensuring it brings about real and lasting change within the organisation. Though this might seem obvious, it is amazing how many tribunals report that an organisation has lost its harassment case because of its failure to ensure that staff are not only aware that a policy exists but are trained to make sure it works in practice. Without training, the 'reasonable steps' defence against harassment claims will almost invariably fail.

Managerial, supervisory and personnel staff are likely to be priorities in this process, as well as those providing independent support and advice via, for example, a confidential helpline. Thought should also be given to incorporating training into existing programmes such as induction training, employee assistance programmes and diversity training.

Training may well start with a general awareness-raising programme, implemented from the top down and encompassing all the stakeholders of the policy. This is likely to do no more than introduce the issues of dignity at work, reinforce the organisation's commitment to tackling these and outline the procedures to be used.

Line managers – so crucial to the effective implementation of any policy – will have the most demanding development needs. Not only will they require thorough and up-to-date knowledge and understanding of the legal framework, the policy itself, and the procedures involved, but they will also need an awareness of how their own attitudes and behaviours may influence those around them and contribute to the success or otherwise of the change process. They will need to be equipped with the skills to deal with a huge range of complex and emotionally charged issues to do with human relationships, social identity and change. The very nature of conflict means situations will usually be unpredictable and difficult to read – successful handling will require a huge degree of sensitivity and emotional intelligence perhaps not seen as a priority in the past. This will be a slow, ongoing process that will require regular reinforcement.

A typical development programme for those who are to be steeped in the policy may start with a several-day intensive learning experience focusing on attitudes and behaviours rather than practices and procedures with many opportunities for reflection, practice, role-play and discussion. Managers should feel able to explore and express their views and to gain confidence in their own ability to handle conflict situations.

Indeed, before they can successfully operate a dignity at work policy, managers might have to take a step back and undertake some more basic diversity training to help them understand not only the business case for diversity but also some of the underlying assumptions and attitudes that create problems in managing a diverse workforce.

The learning points from this intensive session may then be taken back to work and put into practice through managers' everyday activities. This may be backed up by further shorter sessions, perhaps half days, designed to monitor and review progress and deal with particular issues that have arisen. This stage will require close guidance and support from HR and those responsible for implementing the policy to deal with day-to-day needs and questions that arise.

Further specific training may be required in understanding and operating the procedures and practices the policy puts in place, such as conducting interviews, gathering evidence, and running disciplinary or grievance hearings and appeals.

There may also need to be further support for dealing with particular kinds of hearings, such as sexual harassment complaints, race-related complaints, and so on, as these will throw up their own unique issues. Investigating allegations of psychological bullying may require specialist training as it can be extremely subtle and therefore hard to spot and gather evidence on, especially if it has been going on behind closed doors with no witnesses.

Employees will need to consolidate their learning, both formal and informal, perhaps through a further residential course. There will have to be mechanisms for reviewing their learning needs regularly, and this should form a specific part of the appraisals process.

Providing truly independent and unbiased support not only for alleged victims but also alleged perpetrators will require a great deal of expertise and self-knowledge. Those who support and facilitate the policy such as HR, OH and internal counsellors will have their own further development needs, such as formal counselling skills, advocacy skills, and the like, as well as a thorough knowledge and understanding of the issues associated with particular forms of harassment.

London Underground's Ending Harassment programme was built on a network of 'Accredited Managers for Harassment', drawn from all areas of management to deal with formal complaints outside their own business area. They received an initial three days' training followed by six-monthly learning and support days. However, feedback showed this was inadequate and so a much more comprehensive programme was developed which involved six stages, from an initial interview to assess the individual's suitability, through a three-day intensive course, further short courses and briefings, and finally an accreditation day. The applicants are assessed according to seven criteria, i.e. whether they:

1. have a thorough knowledge and understanding of the legal framework

2. have a thorough knowledge and understanding of the company's harassment policy

3. have a thorough knowledge and understanding of different types of discrimination and how they happen

4. understand the sensitivities and difficulties of investigating harassment cases

5. have the ability and courage to make unpopular decisions

6. have the ability to learn continuously

7. have a high standard of interviewing and note-taking skills.

Source: Equal Opportunities Review

MONITORING

Monitoring, evaluating and reviewing policies is important not only to assess their effectiveness but also to ensure that they continuously improve and retain their momentum to bring about the culture change desired.

How and what you monitor will depend largely on the requirements of the organisation, the objectives of the policy and the resources and systems available within the organisation. It can be introduced in stages as resources allow. There are generally three stages in the evaluation process:

1. gathering information

2. analysing the data to identify problems

3. taking action to overcome these problems.

Monitoring and evaluation work best when they are designed into the process of implementation rather than bolted on afterwards. Beginning the process after the project has been put in place may place limits on what can be measured and how. So consulting on and deciding priorities for monitoring and drawing up a programme to achieve these are issues that should be considered by any working group charged with designing and implementing the policy as a whole.

Experts agree that the best approach to evaluation is a mix of qualitative and subjective, and quantitative and objective data but this will depend on who the results are destined for and what they are designed to prove.

Clearly, what questions are asked of the policy depends to a certain extent on what it is intended to achieve. In the unlikely event that a policy is being introduced merely as a defence against legal claims for harassment or bullying or stress, then monitoring the number of claims lodged, won and lost may be sufficient.

If culture change is the aim and raising the trust and morale of the workforce a priority, then repeating the baseline employee opinion surveys on a regular basis will help you decide if attitudes towards conflict issues within the organisation are changing, as well as identifying where the blocks to progress might be. Exit interviews can also be a useful barometer and may highlight particular trouble-spots in one department or even with one manager.

However, taking any one indicator may not give a clear picture. For example, does the company expect or want to see an increase in the number of harassment or bullying complaints reported under the policy or a decrease? An increase in cases may indicate, certainly initially, a greater trust in managers' ability to deal with the problem, perhaps a greater awareness of the problem among staff and an ability to talk about the issue internally. Or it may mean merely that the conflict culture is spreading. At what stage in the evolution of the policy will you expect to see this curve peaking and the number of reports falling? How will you know if this fall in cases indicates a culture shift towards greater tolerance and mutual respect, or a disillusionment with the policy and its ability to solve individual problems?

Hard statistical data will only give a clear picture when combined with more qualitative information, via surveys, face-to-face briefings, regular training and feedback sessions or management reports.

Statistical data could range from merely a log of the number of calls to a harassment helpline or the number of tribunal claims made, to building a customised database analysing cases by different variables such as grade of complainant/complainee, duration of case, grounds for complaint, procedure used, assistance given, or outcome. Where there are specific problems such as race or sexual harassment, cases could also be categorised according to whether there was an element of discrimination.

Note that the decision on how to monitor will have implications for the way in which procedures are carried out and recorded. If a detailed database is planned, for example, it may be necessary for even informal meetings and discussions to be documented with a view to keeping the database complete. It may also necessitate extra training, as note-taking in such sensitive and complex cases is often far from easy.

Any records will be subject to the strict conditions laid down by the Data Protection Act 1998. Much of the data involved will come under the heading of 'sensitive personal data'. This consists of information about an employee's:

- racial or ethnic origins

- political opinions

- religious beliefs

- trade union membership (or non-membership)

- physical or mental health or condition

- sex life or sexual orientation

- criminal (or alleged criminal) activities

- criminal proceedings, criminal convictions or sentences.

Sensitive personal data must not be held on file without the individual's express consent – unless it is held in compliance with an employer's legal obligations (for example under health and safety legislation) or to protect the employee's vital interests (for example under the Sex Discrimination Act 1975). This exception will clearly apply to some of the data held on a dignity at work policy database, but probably not all of it. Even so, it must only be retained for so long as may be necessary for the purpose, say, of defending a complaint of unlawful discrimination on grounds of sex, race, disability or trade union membership (or non-membership), or, so long as appropriate safeguards are in place, for reviewing, monitoring, promoting or maintaining the employer's equal opportunities policy.

Therefore, where a detailed database is planned, there must be mechanisms for gaining employee consent where necessary, and for reviewing the data regularly to ensure it can still justifiably be retained. It may be appropriate to consider holding all the information in an anonymous form so that individuals cannot be identified.

MAINTAINING MOMENTUM

Maintaining the momentum for change and the commitment of staff and especially managers is vital to ensuring any dignity at work policy becomes woven into the fabric of the organisation. The monitoring and evaluation process should do this by assuring managers that they are not alone and that difficulties in operating the policy will be listened to and worked on, by helping to identify areas where there might be resistance to change and concentrating effort there, and by deciding where to reinforce the messages through further training or communication exercises.

Finally, more general human capital reporting measures such as staff turnover, sickness absence, and productivity, may also be valuable indicators of whether a policy is having the desired effect on morale, stress levels and employee commitment. Though establishing immediate cause and effect may be difficult, evidence that the culture change programme may be helping to save recruitment costs and days lost and improving efficiency will undoubtedly help maintain senior management's attention during the long haul.

Chapter Seven
Conflict Management Training

Mike Bagshaw

INTRODUCTION

Conflicts in the workplace are increasing in number and intensity. This has a huge cost in terms of emotions, lost business, time, and straight demands for money from litigation. Arbitration goes some way to easing this, but is still time-consuming and costly. Accepting an arbitrator also means you have to accept his or her decision, so there is a loss of control over the outcome. Mediation keeps those involved in the arena. The mediator does not draw conclusions on their behalf, but assists in the struggle towards resolution. This may bring a good solution to the current problems, but does not necessarily have any impact on future problems.

It is too much to hope that no more contentious issues will arise, so the long-term solution has to be to empower everyone to 'nip things in the bud' by resolving their own disputes and differences as they emerge. It is like teaching someone to drive, rather than giving them a lift.

REACTIONS AND ATTITUDES TO CONFLICT

Conflict exists on many levels, from friendly banter to vicious sniping. There's a difference between the inevitable differences about how people see things, and bitter raging of battles and mutual hatred. Disagreement will happen, but if it is well managed it need not develop into warfare.

People at work often find it particularly hard to deal with difficult issues arising from differences in opinion or needs. We tend to either avoid or ignore the conflict, 'brushing it under the carpet' or go in blazing. Neither approach is helpful.

A divergence in views can create friction, as it's uncomfortable having someone contradict what you say. However, if you suppress the friction by keeping quiet, your ideas never get heard. You can't have creativity without new ideas. You can't have new ideas without disagreement of some sort. Positive conflict occurs when two or more people with differing views say what they think, with their ears wide open to discover what the others can add. 'Add' is important here. In negative conflict, admitting the other person's view will subtract from your own. In positive conflict, extra views are a bonus.

Conflict management is an essential part of the way forward. This means recognising that there is (and always will be) some conflict, and learning to deal with it in an open, respectful, and emotionally intelligent way.

	Conflict avoidance	**Conflict management**
Behaviour	Backbiting Keeping secrets Aggression Fighting to win Guarded communication	Bringing out the issues Being open with information Assertiveness Looking for solutions Open communication
Feelings	Resentment Distrust Anxiety Apathy Antipathy	Respect Trust Confidence Enthusiasm Friendship
Performance	Weary Poor decisions Low morale	Energetic Good decisions High morale
Effect on team	Competitive with each other Energy for victory over others Hiding information	Collaborative Energy for creative solutions Sharing information
Result	**Stagnation**	**Growth**

The good news is that we can all learn to deal with disagreement more effectively. Part of that learning is addressing the myths of conflict.

First, think about whether you agree or disagree with the following statements:

1. You've got to be friends with the people you work with.

2. Anger is an enemy and must be vanquished.

3. Every conflict has a solution.

4. If you don't solve it immediately, it will just get worse.

5. Good management prevents conflicts in the first place.

6. When there is conflict, somebody has to back down.

7. If you ignore conflict, it will blow over.

8. Properly committed people don't waste time with conflict.

9. You can't have communication between angry people.

10. You have to let anger out.

Now read the facts about conflict.

MYTH ONE – You've got to be friends with the people you work with

A work team isn't a cosy gathering of friends who pat each other on the back and agree all the time. It's a group of people who have organised themselves to get a job done. They should be selected for their abilities in different areas, so that between them they have all the skills necessary for the particular project. They might not choose each other as holiday companions: that doesn't matter as long as they respect each other and are prepared to listen and contribute. There are many people whose views you value, but you don't want to be with them longer than is necessary to obtain their services.

This doesn't mean it's OK if they hate each other. If there is real animosity, it could block progress to achieving team goals. It's in the nature of discussion that there will be more than one viewpoint, and it's important that the people present genuinely accept this, and do not resent anyone else for their opinions. Conflict management is essential.

MYTH TWO – Anger is an enemy and must be vanquished

Anger is natural. It has evolved to give us energy to defend ourselves under threat. It's damaging to lash out, even with the tongue, but the energy can be harnessed into getting things changed. When people are angry, but avoid vengeful words or action in favour of seeking a solution, it can be the spur to real progress. Anger can rise quickly, and do a lot of damage in a short time. People need to be able to cool themselves before they act. It's important to look at the cause, and tackle that, rather than dismiss the anger as bad in itself.

MYTH THREE – Every conflict has a solution

You will sometimes meet irresolvable differences. This doesn't matter as long as the people involved accept that others have a different way of looking at things. If they respect each other, it is fine to agree to differ.

MYTH FOUR – If you don't solve it immediately, it will just get worse

Ill feeling is so unpleasant that it's tempting to try to get all parties to resolve it immediately. It's rarely possible. A quick decision usually leaves some, if not all parties dissatisfied. There may need to be a cooling off period so everyone can tackle the problem in a calm state of mind. This also gives the opportunity to seek out any necessary information. At the beginning, it's better to focus on what alternatives might be possible, rather than trying to find one right solution.

MYTH FIVE – Good management prevents conflicts in the first place

The only way to eradicate conflict is to eradicate free thought. Autocratic management can push it out of sight, but it will simmer beneath the surface and may erupt. Meanwhile, there are hidden ideas that could lead to creative solutions. Good management positively encourages these ideas to come out, while establishing a climate of trust and openness, so that a variety of ideas can develop.

MYTH SIX – When there is conflict, somebody has to back down

It is rarely a case of one thing or another. If the parties get together to discuss common ground, they are likely to find a solution where everyone gets some of what they want. This is the win–win approach.

MYTH SEVEN – If you ignore conflict, it will blow over

There are some disagreements that are too small and unimportant to remain after a night's sleep. There are many others that will grow quietly to enormous proportions if they are allowed to fester. Good management will recognise which conflicts can be safely left, and which must be tackled at an early stage. Some unpleasantness now might avert a battle later.

MYTH EIGHT – Properly committed people don't waste time with conflict

Properly committed people will have strong feelings about goals and the ways to achieve them. They will come up with different ideas, and there will be disagreement. If there is never any conflict, it suggests the team members don't really care.

MYTH NINE – You can't have communication between angry people

Communication between angry people is super-efficient. It's also destructive and focuses strongly on the negative, whether it takes the form of slanging matches, sarcasm, subtle put-downs, petty revenge or ostracism. It's important to change this to communication that will help people to move forward.

MYTH TEN – You have to let anger out

Feelings of fury are often so strong that it seems the only way to get rid of it is to let it out. This is a poor policy. The more you practise being angry, the better you will get at it, and the more difficult you will find it to express your viewpoint in other ways. It's important to be able to point that you feel the wrong direction is being taken, but damaging to do this with any form of attack.

BARRIERS TO CONFLICT MANAGEMENT

How do we get across to each other that we disagree, without either attacking the views of another person or feeling that our own views are under attack? How can we ensure that discussions on points of disagreement remain focused on the issues, and do not degenerate into scoring points or denigrating personalities?

There are four main barriers to constructive conflict management that may need to be addressed with training and development.

- *Communication* – People stop listening, and stop being aware of non-verbal cues. They state their own view, and reject information provided by others. They constantly misinterpret. They may stop speaking all together.

- *Procedures* – It may be difficult to communicate effectively simply because of the structure of the organisation. There may too many people, so it's hard to know who to contact. The appropriate people may leave the organisation, or there may be standard procedures that slow things down.

- *Personal concerns* – Individuals may be fighting for personal goals, like status or a particular hobby-horse.

- ***Anxiety*** – Discovering somebody disagrees with you may make you feel your world is under threat. A mature and well-managed team will recognise these feelings for what they are, and the discomfort will pass. If not, minor tension can escalate into personal battles. This can create great problems later, when people need to renegotiate their relationship so they can continue working together, or some people will have to leave

In addition, four elements create and exacerbate tension in teams:

- ***Blame*** – Nobody wants to be blamed, and to find somebody else to take it can seem like a quick fix. This can lead on to a culture where finding out who is culpable is more important than finding a solution of mutual benefit.

- ***Secrecy*** – This is often the result of a blame culture. In order to avoid blame, people are careful to conceal any errors they make. They get defensive and stick to their first response because consistency seems important in defending themselves. Others in the group are also defending themselves, but taking a different stance. There follows a battle between stances, which has little to do with the issues they started with.

- ***Bottling up*** – Anger can be bottled up for a while, but it will eventually break out with great force. Meanwhile the protagonists are likely to go for other ploys such as sarcastic remarks or deliberate slow working. This is not to say they should let things out in an uncontrolled rage. The proper alternative to bottling up is to state their views in a calm and respectful way.

- ***Anger*** – May be exploded without damage if it is extremely brief, and is immediately followed by suggestions for resolution. This is better than allowing it to fester until it is a canker that cannot be cured, but falls short of the ideal of airing opposing views as they occur, within a respectful relationship.

THE LANGUAGE OF CONFLICT

The words we use can have a strong effect on how we feel about conflict. Metaphors particularly have a striking effect. Seeing conflict as a war may make us feel bellicose before we start. Seeing it as a gateway will give us a more positive mindset.

Conflict as war

Competition for business can get fierce and lead to other organisations being regarded as the enemy. There may be strategic planning to put obstacles in their way, even with a view to forcing them out. This attitude sometimes spills over inside the organisation. Instead of trusting and collaborating, employees compete against their own colleagues. They may all achieve greater success, personal as well as corporate, if they worked constructively together.

Conflict as gateway

When someone disagrees with you they are offering you a new way of seeing things, which could be a gateway to a new path to success. Seeing it like this will prevent animosity towards the person who's disagreeing, so it won't be an obstacle to collaboration.

Conflict as safari

A safari is a journey where travelling towards the objective is as important as arriving. It might not always be comfortable, but is an enriching part of the experience. Making a safari to a business goal via dialogue, debate and decisions can make the inevitable conflict seem like a stimulating part of the journey.

The number of metaphors we can use is limitless. Think about occasions where you are likely to feel like shouting and demanding compliance. Try to think of new metaphors, to open your mind to new ways of looking at the issues, and new ways of dealing with disagreement.

When designing an intervention for conflict management consider how you describe the project.

DESIGNING A CONFLICT MANAGEMENT PROGRAMME

Most people have a baseline of conflict resolution skills. Training will bring these skills to the surface and polish them. Training also gives the opportunity to learn techniques for coping, without the risk of bad consequences for getting it wrong.

The specific training required for any organisation depends on its line of business, the skills its employees need and the deficits that exist. Conflict management training is different: it goes across the board. Conflict can descend on any organisation, whatever its type, with similar results.

The conflict management trainer doesn't have to be an expert in all the research and background theory. However, he or she does need to be a competent facilitator who can draw out discussion about experience and feelings. Strong emotion is likely to come to the surface, so the facilitator does need sensitivity. He or she needs to be able to move around the group, sensing the 'emotional landscape' rather than setting an exercise and stepping back.

Conflict management programmes should not be about 'opening up.' That would not be an emotionally intelligent thing to do. They should be about trying to develop sensitivity, skill and new perspectives, so that people can manage conflict to gain better working relationships, more involvement and innovation, and thereby more satisfied customers and value for money.

Managing conflict is not like learning to ride a bike. Once you have the skill, you can ride a bike any time at all, no matter how long it has been since you last did it. Conflict management, on the other hand, involves a set of skills, insights and beliefs that needs continuous sharpening and re-addressing.

You will increase the effectiveness of your programme if you address the following questions.

What skills does the organisation need to acquire?

Training is essentially a preventative approach to conflict. Everyone in the organisation should therefore benefit from basic skills training to enable them to deal with the inevitable problems and disagreements that, if badly managed, can lead to escalating conflict. This includes general communication skills such as effective listening, combined with a degree of training in how to control and deal with emotion. A well facilitated programme involving carefully managed role-plays (perhaps using actors) in listening and problem-solving skills exercises can help people to manage everyday conflicts more effectively as they arise.

But this is not an ideal world, and sometimes training is required to help those who are already having to deal with more serious levels of conflict. The chart summarises the different stages of a conflict and the interventions that may be necessary at each one.

At levels two and three, there may be a need for trained internal mediators to handle disputes that those involved are finding difficult to resolve themselves. The training issue is then to ensure internal mediators are equipped with more circumscribed professional mediation techniques.

At levels four and five there may be a need to call in external professional help. The internal training issue may be when to refer the problem to external professionals and then how to rebuild trust and morale in the team afterwards.

If we are able to create a climate where people can address levels one and two effectively then there will be less level three, four and five conflicts with all the attendant costs and risks. Training can play a significant part in achieving this.

Conflict Level Chart

	Level One Problem	Level Two Dispute	Level Three Contest	Level Four Combat	Level Five Insoluble
	It is advisable to train everyone in organisation to deal with Level One conflicts	*Those who are expected to deal with Levels Two and Three will need additional training, probably in mediation skills*		*Conflicts that reach Level Four or Five call for more professional assistance usually from outside the organisation*	
Focus	Focus is on the problem, not on personalities	Begins to get personal Negative politics begin Issues blurred	Personal attacks Resistance to ideas from other side	Desire to remove opponent	Original cause is forgotten and personalities are blamed
Feelings	Quick bursts of anger, soon over Discomfort in each other's presence	Anger goes deeper Beginning to mistrust	Dislike meeting opposing faction	Self-justification Actively avoid other parties, sometimes ostracism	Obsessive pursuit of own desired result Conclusions are subjective
Language	Direct and clear	Some sideways remarks	Generalisation Use of 'always' 'never'	Moves into ideologies 'It's a matter of principle'	Words like 'remove' and 'sack' are readily used
Information	People share information readily	They begin to be guarded about what they disclose	Information gets distorted in argument	Information only accepted if it backs the view of the disputant	Information is adapted as required to back up the case of the disputant
Goal	To reach agreement	Consensus, but with protection of pride	To defeat the opposition	To expel the opposing faction	Vengeful action
Likely Outcome	Win-win Mutually acceptable solution	Still want win-win, but needs more effort	Find solution by voting, compromise or mediation	High risk of people walking out, maybe leaving the organisation	Outside decision/ arbitration and compulsory enforcement

	Level One **Problem**	Level Two **Dispute**	Level Three **Contest**	Level Four **Combat**	Level Five **Insoluble**
	All skills required at a lower level are also required at a higher level. Level One skills are needed at all levels. Level Two skills are needed for Level Two conflicts and above, etc.				
Skills	Trust Rapport building Active listening Consultation Problem-solving Decision-making Knowledge of resources available	Analytical skills Self-awareness Understanding of dynamics of power and influence in the organisation Negotiation skills Deeper level empathy	Mediation skills Recognising the limits of mediation Understanding of how different types of personalities interact Facilitation skills Developing the process of decision-making Designing contracts	High level of previous experience Knowledge of outside resources Willingness to acquire higher level skills as part of professional role Circumscribed interventions e.g. cognitive behavioural techniques	Strong inner self Resources for personal support and supervision Stress management skills Knowledge of legal aspects of disputes
Training	Group training using presentations and skills practice with feedback Role-play Case studies	Facilitated workshops on real issues Advanced skills training courses Deeper level drama techniques	Mediation training Longer-term development Use of Psychometrics One-to-one coaching	Realisation of when it's time to find a settlement, rather than resolving the issue Knowing when a specialist is needed	All round giving of support Plan for rebuilding of relationships Post trauma issues Legal

What is required to achieve excellence in the job?

This can be done through formal job assessment approaches and the design of competency frameworks. It can also be done informally by observation, inquiry and discussion. Try to tease out the conflict management elements that will make the difference. This will enable you to enrich the activities with real life, relevant examples, and will aid learning transfer.

How ready are the participants?

Conflict management training may require a greater level of openness and depth than is usual in training programmes. Some people may find this uncomfortable. You can encourage greater openness and disclosure if you establish a confidentiality contract. Assure the participants that the goal is not to force people to open up, but to provide an opportunity for people to share experiences in a helpful way.

Bear in mind that some people may be particularly vulnerable or resistant to this kind of training. It might be helpful to arrange one-to-one sessions where they can express their concerns and anxieties. You may have to brief line managers to do the same if there are participants from far afield and unknown to you. Bear in mind that in demonstrating this kind of sensitivity, you are modelling aspects of emotional intelligence.

What are the target group's current conflict styles?

As a starting point it may be useful to assess the way your target group typically deals with conflict.

The Thomas-Kilman Conflict Mode Instrument (TKI) is a self-scoring assessment tool that can be completed in ten minutes. The results show which of five styles the individual is likely to use when dealing with conflict.

The five styles are:

- **Competing** – Aiming for a win-lose result by whatever tactics necessary.

- **Accommodating** – Accepting lose-win – conceding everything and sacrificing their own viewpoint to escape from the conflict situation.

- **Collaborating** – Aiming for win-win solutions, by sharing information and ideas, and discussing differences openly, trying to find the common ground so both parties can win.

- **Compromising** – Looking for solutions where both parties win a little and lose a little.

- **Avoiding** – Burying their head in the sand and denying the problem exists, in the hope it will disappear.

Although the collaborative approach is the most effective in most situations, there are times when the other styles are appropriate. Also, there are effective ways of using each style. This kind of analysis can form the basis of a practical skills-based learning session.

How do you reinforce the learning?

Conflict management is not a 'one-off hit'. You need to continuously reinforce the key principles in other development programmes.

How do you choose the right training organisation?

Collaboration and consensus-building develop from the basic skills of negotiation, mediation and facilitation. These are essential skills in modern business and there is a wide range of courses available, with a variety of focuses – you have to make sure the course you choose is right for your needs. One way to choose a course is to go for the trainer first, then ask questions:

- Does this trainer understand the culture of your organisation?

- Will their training be relevant to practical issues?

- Do they strike the right balance between theory and practice?

- Can they inspire the staff?

Courses may last a few hours, or several weeks. Short courses tend to focus on mediation and negotiation; they also help the decision-makers to decide who is suitable for further training.

Longer courses develop into facilitation skills training, allowing participants to explore the more complex variables that come into play in conflict situations. This could cover cultural contrasts and ethical dilemmas.

Another decision is whether to send employees on public courses, or to bring trainers in house. The latter has the benefit of being tailored to suit your organisation.

How do you brief the trainer?

It is very important to brief the training organisation carefully. For example, it is a good idea to work with the trainer to design case studies representative of the types of conflicts and stakeholder positions your staff routinely face.

TRAINING METHODOLOGIES

When designing effective training interventions we need to consider the two basic aspects of the self: the cognitive self and the experiential self.

Our **cognitive self** is with us most of the time, and we are conscious of the thoughts and processes that make us the way we are. It is formed from the summation of our learning from early life to the present. When in cognitive mode, we assess the situation and make rational decisions based on what we believe to be best.

Our **experiential self** is below the surface. It also comes from learning, but at an unconscious level. It brings us less rational, more knee-jerk reactions, for reasons we may not understand. It may be the result of early experience of disapproval, too unpleasant to remember, but we still feel the effects. We have all asked ourselves the question: *'What on earth made me do that?'*.

Most of the time, the cognitive self overrides the experiential self. In times of stress and conflict, however, it can be the other way round and we react to events from the standpoint of long-forgotten experiences.

These unconscious schemata are very resistant to change. They need to be superseded by new learning, and the heat of bitter conflict is not the right time. Training can be directed toward both the cognitive and experiential selves, but is most likely to be effective if it focuses on the experiential self.

The following methods can be used singly or together to meet your specific training requirements.

Lectures and presentations

Trainers present factual material in a direct, logical manner – for example, some data on the costs of specific conflicts in the workplace. You can also use the lecture format to present inspiring stories about how conflicts have been resolved. The more these stories are drawn from real situations of the kind experienced in your organisation, the better.

This method is quite useful for large groups, especially if you need to set the context for dealing positively with conflict.

One problem is that the audience tends to be rather passive and communication is predominantly one way. At the very least, it is helpful to engage the audience in discussion or break into groups to discuss experiences or apply the theory inputs to their own circumstances. Time constraints may affect discussion opportunities.

Trainers also need to be skilled at asking appropriate questions and 'shifting gears' quickly.

The effectiveness of learning is also difficult to gauge – it can be a bit of a scattergun approach.

Case studies

Case studies involve more participation and allow learners to explore possible solutions to complex issues and apply new knowledge and thinking tools. For example, a case study may be the basis for inviting participants to apply their knowledge of conflict resolution options. A danger is that the participants may not see any relevance to their own situations; this can be avoided if the case study material is carefully prepared and drawn from real experiences of conflict in your organisation.

Case studies are more about head than heart. Given that the emotional aspect of conflicts is so powerful, this can be a serious limitation. However, they can be snippets of real experience, from which we can learn the benefits and pitfalls of a particular approach. The participants can then simulate dealing with the case in reality. They can meet in small groups first to talk about the case. Then, with the facilitator as guide, they can work through the process – identifying the problem, analysing cause and effect, thinking about alternative ways forward, and finally recommending a course of action.

A case study could be used, for example, to show a confrontational attitude that didn't work. Participants are often sure they know how it should have been handled, and during the course of the discussion are often surprised to find the range of opinion that emerges. This gives them practice in listening and thinking about alternatives. It is an example of taking on board different opinions, while working towards an agreed action.

Role-play

Role-playing can introduce conflict scenarios in a more dramatic way. It provides the opportunity for participants to assume others' roles and thus appreciate other points of view while allowing solutions to be explored.

Role-playing also provides the opportunity to practise skills, though some participants may feel too self-conscious or threatened. This method is not generally appropriate for large groups. The trainer needs to define the conflict situation and roles first and give very clear instructions.

Role-playing exercises add realism to the training. They can be based on genuine situations, and participants can try different approaches in the safety of the training room both to managing their own conflicts and to mediating. The trainer could first cover the early stages – from where the conflict began to stir, through to the process of setting up mediation, and then establishing ground rules. Role-play could begin at the point where the ground rules have been established.

Drama techniques

Drama is a way of putting us in touch with our feelings. In the context of training, it can be the basis of a learning experience in which people can face situations that would frighten them in real life. It can increase their awareness of their skills and give them the chance to try different approaches and styles, make mistakes, and try again.

Drama-based training can be designed to have a low, medium or high impact:

- **Low impact**
  The aim of low impact drama training is to introduce a topic, such as diversity, with a view to increasing awareness and encouraging discussion. Actors perform a short play which raises important issues. It may or may not be modified to suit the particular organisation. There is a facilitator who introduces the topic, answers questions and guides a general discussion at the end. This level of training is good for raising awareness in large numbers of people. It tends not to address deeper levels of feeling and attitude.

- **Medium impact**
  This goes beyond general awareness and includes audience participation, in a way that encourages thinking about motivation and behaviour. The scenarios are usually adapted to the concerns of the particular organisation. The audience can ask the actors questions about their motivation and attitude, which they will answer as the character they are playing. Sometimes, the audience divides into small groups for discussion with one of the actors. This may result in changes to the scenario, to explore different aspects of the issues.

  The extra involvement can considerably heighten awareness, and the issues can be explored in depth. It does, however, require more time than low impact training.

- **High impact**

  In this form of training the audience is immersed in the experience. It gives participants the chance to experiment with different styles of conflict management and mediation, without the repercussions of getting it wrong. In conflict mediation people only get the chance to practise their skills in sensitive situations which need to be handled right. High-impact drama training gives them a chance to experiment in safety.

  The scenarios are created to reflect the relevant issues and the context in which they occur. They are also geared to specific work experience and learning needs. The audience interacts directly with the actors, so scenarios can be adjusted as they go along to ensure maximum relevance. This can only work well with small audiences – an absolute maximum of 25.

Playback

Playback is a high impact improvisational technique in which audience stories are played back on the spot by an ensemble of trained actors. Two or more actors play a scenario, then the facilitator asks the audience for their views on what happens next. The audience can also suggest alternative courses of action which the actors then play out. This requires experienced and skilled actors, but it can be a very powerful way of illuminating the emotional undercurrents of conflict.

Workplace conference

A workplace conference is a meeting where people discuss an event that has caused harm. It is allied to family therapy, where family members talk about issues and attempt to achieve mutual congruence.

In the workplace conference, the people who feel aggrieved meet with those who have aggrieved them, along with their supporters, and a convenor, and sometimes those who have investigated the event. They sit in a circle, and have equal status in the conference.

Those involved describe the event and how it affected them *(story telling phase)*, which usually leads to new realisations, apologies and forgiveness *(healing phase)*. This follows on to a written agreement *(learning phase)* which they all sign. There is a high success rate, both in stopping the behaviour and in restoring good relationships.

The workplace conference has important differences from the legal process and from mediation. The legal process centres on facts, and the disputants are expected to accept decisions. Mediation concentrates on finding mutually acceptable solutions, but discourages the expression of strong feeling for fear it will disrupt the progress towards resolution.

In the workplace conference, each party has others present who support their view. This is a tacit way of reaffirming their case and reducing the need for them to repeat themselves, so outbursts are less likely.

Emotions form part of disputes. The legal process typically creates resentment as emotions are given passing consideration, if any. Mediation does accept emotions are there, but the purpose is to get past them to a solution. The workplace conference gives people the opportunity to express the emotional effects of the situation, with support. This tends to bring deeper realisation of what has been happening and why. Those present gain deeper understanding, and are more likely to be genuinely sorry or forgiving. This gives a basis for rebuilding in the future. People who have been locked in bitter dispute have more chance of working successfully together, rather than avoiding each other.

NEGOTIATION SKILLS TRAINING

Negotiation is probably the main set of skills associated with conflicts. It is a process whereby two or more people with a mutual interest try to find common ground. There is rarely a solution where everyone is completely satisfied, but the process can be considered a success if they reach an agreement where all those involved have won something for themselves. If there is a clear victor it is probably not negotiation but brow-beating.

For successful negotiation you need to:

- identify the range of objectives

- be open to alternative ways forward

- come with a willingness to be flexible

- listen actively to what others are saying

- ask questions without anticipating the answers

- set priorities in what you really want, and where you can yield

- see the advantages in allowing others to have part of what they want.

Principles of negotiation

Overcoming obstacles

Negotiation does not seek victory over the other parties. It is a technique for taking things forward when there are different perspectives. There are three obstacles to this – perception, emotion and communication.

- **Perception**

  There may be preconceptions about what the other party thinks, preventing real listening. It's best to lay existing beliefs on the table at the outset. If you feel assumptions are being made about your beliefs, you can express things in a different way. This is less provocative than straight contradiction. You can also show you are listening to them, by trying to describe the situation in their terms. This gives a valid framework for discussion.

- **Emotion**

  Negative emotions are powerful and contagious. One angry person rapidly infects the whole room. It can be neutralised by bringing it into the open. Saying *'I feel ...'* gives the right standpoint. Recognising and accepting the feelings of others is also important. If someone says they feel angry, don't try to conquer them. Acknowledge the anger and the reasons, and discuss calmly.

- **Communication**

  Good negotiators listen. They don't just pause to allow others to speak while they rehearse their next point. They also make their own points as clearly as they can.

Meeting our own interests

Interests are not the same as positions. Interests are what we see as important. Positions are the ways we think our interests can be met. Sometimes, positions get rigid. It's important to consider whether the suggestions being made might lead to our interests being met just as well as our own position.

SOCIAL INTERACTION TRAINING

There are many jobs that invite conflict – for example, where members of the public often feel frustrated, such as in a benefits office, or where alcohol is involved.

In these jobs forewarned is forearmed, and employees can be trained in how to defuse potentially difficult situations. A range of training techniques are used to develop skills for dealing with specific situations. For example, the following practical points may help the employee avoid a potentially dangerous escalation of hostility and aggression.

Ways of handling aggression

Keep calm	It may be tempting to give as good as you get, but it will make things worse.
Calm the person	If they are clearly in a state, calm them first. They won't listen while they are shrieking.
Be clear	Tell them exactly what you will insist on. If they must leave, make sure they do. If being quiet is enough, keep on saying that, then be satisfied.
Keep personalities out of it	Stress that it is the behaviour that is unacceptable. Don't make personal criticisms.
Make it clear what you can and cannot do	If it's not in your power to do what they ask, say so. It may help them think about alternatives.
Don't aim for victory	People are more likely to be calm if a compromise is offered. Aim for a win–win situation.
Allow face-saving	However tempting it is to put the aggressor down, it will only increase their anger.

An example of a straightforward social interaction training programme took place in New York. Four white police officers shot Amadou Diallo, a West African, and were convicted of murder. Protests about police brutality followed and over a thousand people were arrested. It did lead to positive action, however: New York Police are now issued with cards containing basic advice about respecting individuals and being polite – for example by saying 'please' and 'thank you'. This is very basic stuff for defusing conflicts. Social interaction training can give a huge boost to these relationships, which by their nature invite conflict. The training includes such areas as active listening, introspection and body language, as well as mediation skills. Police can learn to resolve disputes in a way that makes it less likely that a difficult situation will escalate into violence. This leads to improved relationships between the police and the public and avoids arrests, court cases and penalties.

CONCLUSION

Conflict is an inevitable part of life, but battle is not. Conflict resolution is a viable alternative. It's not about giving in, or avoiding issues. It's about finding answers that satisfy all parties and point the way forward. The fact of conflict shows there is room for more than one opinion; when this is accepted and managed, it can enrich the discussion and lead to innovation. Without conflict, we would have stagnation. With conflict badly managed, we have hostility. With conflict well managed, we have growth.

Too many organisations have no policy at all regarding conflict, thinking it will take care of itself. Once hostility gets a hold, it takes on a life of its own. Protagonists compete to best the latest humiliation, or strenuously avoid each other. Both are destructive, both to individuals and to organisations.

Nothing will be gained by reciting platitudes that nobody hears. Rebukes and exhortations to grow up will further stoke up the fire. Instead it is essential to acknowledge the needs of the people involved, and those on the periphery.

Conflict training will arouse emotions. It will be difficult to deal with these, especially when they reflect key issues, as they need to do. Trainers are as reluctant as anyone else to face these situations. But it is important to do so, as conflict management is essential to effective teamworking, and effective teamworking is essential for successful business.

REFERENCES AND RESOURCES

Books

Constructive Conflict	John Crawley, 1992, Nicholas Brearley Publishing
Emotional Intelligence	Daniel Goleman, 1996, Bloomsbury
Working with Emotional Intelligence	Daniel Goleman, 1993, Bloomsbury
Getting to Yes	Roger Fisher and Ury, Boston, 1981, Houghton Mifflin
People Skills: How to Assert Yourself, Listen to Others and Resolve Conflicts	Robert Bolton, 1980, Prentice-Hall

Everyone Can Win: *How to Resolve Conflict*	Helena Cornelius, Shoshana Faire, 1994, Simon & Schuster
The Mediation Process: *Practical Strategies for* *Resolving Conflict*	Christopher W Moore, 2003, Jossey–Bass, Wiley
Getting to Resolution	Stewart Levine, 1998, Berrett–Koehler

Trainer's materials

Thomas-Kilmann Conflict Mode Instrument

Distributed in Europe by Management Learning Resources Ltd, PO Box28, Carmarthen, SA31 1DT, UK

Dealing with Difficult and Aggressive Behaviour: Build Your People's Skills and Confidence in Managing Conflict (Trainer's Activity Packs.)

Caroline Love, Fenman Training, 1999

Using Emotional Intelligence at Work: 17 tried and tested activities for understanding the practical application of emotional intelligence (Trainer's Activity Packs.)

Fenman Training, Dr Mike Bagshaw, 2000

The Conflict Resolution Training Program: Leader's Manual

Pfeiffer, Prudence B. Kestner, Larry Ray; ISBN: 0787960772

Training Games for Assertiveness and Conflict Resolution: 50 Ready-to-use Activities

McGraw-Hill Education; ISBN: 0079130526, 1996

Conflict Management Workshop: A Trainers Guide (The Trainer's Workshop Series)

Bill Withers, Amacom; ISBN: 0814470920, 2002

The Conflict Resolution Training Program: Participant's Workbook

Prudence B. Kestner, Larry Ray, Jossey Bass Wiley, 2002

Website resources

Resolving Conflict in the Workplace

http://www.idiotsguides.com/Quick-Guides/MG_Conflict_Work-place/file.htm

Conflict Management

www.work911.com/conflict/index.htm

Several sites listed: Addressing Interpersonal Conflict

http://www.mapnp.org/library/intrpsnl/conflict.htm

Learn2.com

Learn2.com offers a wide variety of online courses in conflict resolution, negotiation and more. Some of the courses offered include:

- Conflict Resolution

- Effective Negotiation

- Confronting and Resolving Conflict

- Conflict Management.

Basic Mediation Training – Trainers' Guide

http://www.campus-adr.org/CR_Services_Cntr/mit.html
Free resource but read conditions of use on the website.

http://www.trans4mation.com
The author's website. Includes free articles on conflict and related areas.

http://www.theraidinstitute.com
The RAID Institute is an independent organisation that provides training for this working with people who display extreme behaviour.

Chapter Eight

Reaching Agreement in Cases of Conflict: The Role of Mediation

Dave Liddell

INTRODUCTION

Mediation, one of the principal pillars of alternative dispute resolution (ADR), is playing an increasingly important role in all aspects of our lives. Civil law, business and commercial law, family law, criminal law, community relations and increasingly employment relations are all embracing the values and approaches of mediation.

From a workplace perspective it is widely acknowledged that modern organisations have people at the very heart of their processes and their practices, and are realising new levels of competitiveness by harnessing the creativity and energy of a diverse and dynamic workforce. However, these benefits are often eroded and undermined by unresolved, bitter and hostile workplace conflicts. The considerable costs of conflict are extensively covered within this book (see **CHAPTER 3**).

Mediation is still in its infancy yet already many organisations are recognising that mediation offers a new approach that allows firms to regain their competitive advantage and offer best value by enabling their staff to resolve their disputes speedily, effectively and productively.

Many employers are now committed to bringing these benefits to their workplaces, thereby establishing a prevailing culture of communication, collaboration and competitiveness.

Case study

Anita and Sarah had been in dispute for almost six months. Their incessant bickering and arguments were a regular feature of the office and had become an almost 'normal' part of their working lives. Yet no one in their team would describe their relationship as anything other than damaging, destructive and harmful. Their conflict was becoming a major source of anxiety and stress for everyone.

One day Anita appeared in the office looking upset and angry. She and Sarah had just met in the corridor and engaged in a strongly worded altercation. Anita felt that Sarah had over stepped the mark by calling her a 'lazy cow'. Sarah on the other hand felt deeply aggrieved by Anita's sarcastic and aggressive attitude. Sarah approached her manager Peter to raise her grievance. After listening to Sarah, Peter decided that the time had come to settle the dispute once and for all. That afternoon Peter met Anita and Sarah separately and recommended that they both sit down and talk to a mediator.

A few days later, the mediator, at separate confidential meetings, gave Anita and Sarah the chance to outline their perspectives on the conflict. The mediator explained that his role was to listen to both sides, not to judge who was right or wrong, and to help them explore their differences and try to agree on a solution with which they would both be satisfied. Anita and Sarah seemed happy with the mediator's role; in fact they both stated that this is just what they had needed for a long time.

During the initial meetings, Anita and Sarah described their conflict in detail; they also outlined their goals for mediation. Both parties felt a lot better just being given the chance to 'offload' and be heard. Once the mediator had met both sides they had a much clearer idea of what was wrong. However, the mediator was quick to remember that it was not for them to determine a solution: their role was to facilitate a discussion between Sarah and Anita to help them find one for themselves.

The mediator sought a neutral venue for both parties to meet each other and a mediation meeting was arranged. At the start of the mediation, the mediator established some clear ground rules which would allow both Anita and Sarah to talk openly and respectfully to one another. Initially, both parties felt uncomfortable and anxious but the mediator put them at their ease and invited to them to talk about their experiences.

As they spoke, the other person listened carefully to what was being said. As mediation progressed Anita and Sarah realised that the conflict was actually based on little more than assumptions, misinterpretations and misperceptions. The conversation moved from heated and angry to relaxed and calm. Keen to ensure that no issue was ignored, the mediator encouraged the parties to discuss all of their concerns and feelings openly and frankly. As they talked and listened there were times when their conversation got heated and emotional but never hostile or aggressive.

Towards the end of mediation, the atmosphere began to improve, smiles returned to their faces and they were even able to look at each other in the eyes as they spoke. At one point during mediation, Anita and Sarah reached a moment where they turned to each other and acknowledged that the past six months had been hard for both of them and that the time had come to move on. From then on, mediation was used to focus on the future and to develop a solution that they could both agree on.

Two months later, although they are not best friends, and probably never will be, Anita and Sarah are working together, sharing information and acting professionally and with courtesy towards one another. The reason behind this transformation is simple: they both decided that enough was enough and they decided to settle their differences, not in a corridor but with the aid of a mediator.

Please note that all names have been changed to respect confidentiality.

WHAT IS MEDIATION?

Mediation is a staged process during which a neutral third party works with people in conflict to help them explore and discuss their differences. The mediator helps the parties work towards a constructive resolution of the conflict by encouraging them to identify and agree a range of possible solutions which satisfy some or all of their underlying goals, needs and aspirations. The mediator's role is to:

- Encourage parties to engage in mediation and consider the benefits of discussing their differences and seeking a mutually acceptable resolution.

- Establish a safe and constructive environment in which parties can talk and listen to each other.

- Encourage parties to describe with clarity and purpose how they view the situation and enable them to view it from the other's point of view.

- Help the parties identify and discuss key issues and concerns and encourage parties to use non-violent and non-blaming language.

- Enable the parties to explore a range of options and determine what results would be acceptable.

- Identify ways to help them achieve those results and agree a way forward. Mediators help parties agree on a series of 'do-ables' or 'small steps'.

Mediation is based on the principles of self-determination – the final outcome is agreed by the parties, not imposed by the mediator. Mediators create a 'safe' environment where parties can communicate and work towards the restoration of a positive working relationship.

This is one of the real strengths of mediation – it allows the employee to repair something that has been broken and is potentially damaging. As we saw in previous chapters, conflict left to fester and escalate is often destructive for the parties, their colleagues, their families and the entire organisation. Mediation is one tool available to repair that harm, rebuild relationships and restore a sense of balance and equilibrium. Even in the most extreme cases of workplace conflict, where the situation has resulted in allegations of bullying, harassment and discrimination, mediation may be able to offer a remedy. At its best it is a uniquely restorative process – fair, honest and above all, promoting a sense of real justice for everyone involved.

> "The biggest impact of integrating mediation within our organisation is that it gives more people a constructive opportunity to improve their relationships. It is face saving and gives no sense of loss. It also offers staff a greater choice and it gets to the root of a problem rather than just its outward symptoms. By introducing mediation, it has made people sit up and think about their attitudes and behaviours. It will give them a new way of dealing with conflict....In my view, you constantly learn during mediation, it will help managers manage"
>
> Head of Personnel Services, Croydon Council

The philosophy of mediation

Mediation is underpinned by some powerful factors:

- It encourages disputing parties to settle their disputes out of court.

- It transforms negative conflict into constructive dialogue.

- It encourages parties to take control of the conflict and its resolution.

- It promotes creativity and expression – so often lacking when we are locked in conflict.

- It restores working relationships and acts to prevent further hostility and escalation.

In the workplace, mediation is redefining the way that we respond to conflict by offering a real alternative to traditionally adversarial, confrontational and punitive approaches. Mediation provides an early opportunity to resolve problems and prevent them spiralling out of control – it nips conflict in the bud. It can also offer a credible and face-saving route out of conflict when all else has failed. It gives people an opportunity to re-evaluate their own behaviours and attitudes and seek agreement with colleagues through a safe, structured and constructive process.

The benefits of mediation

Mediation has a broad and diverse range of benefits, many of which can be measured through quantitative means and include reduced costs related to litigation, improved staff retention and reduced absence due to stress-related sickness. However, other benefits are less hard to quantify yet equally as valuable. These include increased levels of self-esteem, team morale and improvements in the psychological, physiological and emotional well-being of employees.

Mediation brings many potential benefits to an organisation:

- It can be applied at any stage of a workplace conflict and it is relatively speedy.

- It is highly cost effective compared with the cost of formal action or an employment tribunal.

- It can reduce levels of stress and sickness absence among employees.

- It offers the opportunity to resolve workplace conflict in a way that meets individuals' and the organisation's needs.

- It is flexible and can accommodate each participant's needs, goals and aspirations.

- It can improve productivity and morale among staff.

- It offers potential remedies to workplace conflict that are not available through adversarial policies and practices.

THE EMERGENCE OF MEDIATION IN THE UK

During the 1980s and 1990s, mediation – between warring neighbours, children in school and in youth justice – became an established and highly credible tool in community relations strategies. Following best practice in New Zealand, the United States and Australia, the UK developed a fairly ad-hoc approach to mediation. At about the same time, mediation was becoming more widely used within the Family Division of the UK court system and was being promoted in a growing number of areas of family and commercial law.

One of the biggest signals for change was in 1994 when the Lord Chancellor, Lord Justice Woolf, was appointed to review the rules and procedures governing the civil courts in England and Wales. The review had two clear aims: to improve access to justice, and to reduce the cost of litigation.

With the publication of the Woolf report, 'Access to Justice' in 1996, it became clear that ADR, and in particular mediation, was about to come of age. The report made clear that the number of cases being brought before the courts was too high and that parties and their lawyers should be encouraged to settle disputes before they came to court. The report pointed directly to mediation as one way of reducing case loads while giving all parties a sense that justice had been done. The government wholeheartedly endorsed Lord Woolf's recommendations and in 1998, they were enacted within the new Civil Procedure Rules (CPR).

Lord Woolf, a passionate advocate of ADR, was highly critical of the cost and burden of litigation, stating:

> 'Mediation is probably the most effective method of resolving disputes without going to trial.'

(*Mediation in Action* by Hazel Genn, foreword by The Right Honourable the Lord Woolf, 1999 CGF)

In parallel with these changes to the legal system, many organisations were starting to change the way they managed working relationships. The proliferation of workplace partnerships, flexible working policies, work–life balance practices, diversity initiatives and employee assistance programmes all presented opportunities for key stakeholders to engage in constructive dialogue and discuss their differences, needs and aspirations.

For many, the traditional ways of managing conflict were no longer acceptable and were being challenged robustly by employees and their representatives alike. This led to a greater tendency for employees to use formal litigation to seek redress.

In October 2001, the government, concerned about the rising numbers of employment tribunal applications, announced a thorough review of the

Employment Tribunal System. In July 2002, the Employment Tribunal System Taskforce published its report, 'Moving Forward'. It made 61 recommendations designed to improve operational efficiency and ensure a coherent approach to strategic planning across the system. In particular, the taskforce recommended greater emphasis on the prevention of litigation through internal dispute resolution schemes, and greater use of external mediation services offering organisations the potential to resolve disputes earlier.

> Alternative dispute resolution approaches have the potential to resolve more disputes at an earlier stage and should therefore, as a general principle, be promoted by the employment Tribunal system and Government more generally. They have potential both as a means to resolve disputes before they reach the system, and to encourage earlier settlement once they do reach the system.

'Moving forward', The Report of the Employment Tribunal Service Taskforce.

Available from: **http://www.dti.gov.uk/er/individual/etst-report.pdf**

Since that time, in accordance with the recommendations of the task force, Total Conflict Management has been establishing a number of mediation schemes in civil service departments, various local authorities, NHS trusts, police forces and several private sector and not-for-profit organisations across the UK. This has involved reviewing internal grievance and disciplinary procedures, training staff in mediation skills, undertaking consultation exercises with key stakeholders and establishing the necessary systems to offer, monitor and evaluate in-house mediation schemes. The overwhelming factor in all of these organisations is an increasing commitment to a greater use of a fair, equitable and productive mechanism in response to workplace conflict.

THE NEW DISPUTE RESOLUTION REGULATIONS

Whilst the government is keen to promote the use of internal dispute resolution and in particular ADR, it has been recognised for some time that more needed to be done to establish a minimum level of dispute resolution regulation to facilitate the resolution of workplace disputes and reduce the increasing number of cases reaching employment tribunal.

This was particularly acute for small business where the DTI identified that employees working (or who worked) in small firms accounted for a disproportionately high share of applications. A third of applications come from people working in firms employing less than ten people. According to the DTI, such firms account for 18% of total employment.

In response to this concern, on 9 July 2003, the DTI published its draft dispute resolution regulations which aim to overhaul dispute resolution procedures and create a statutory minimum level of disciplinary and grievance procedure. From October 2004, there will be a requirement for employers and employees to follow a minimum three-stage process to ensure that disputes are discussed and hopefully resolved at work.

The process will require:

1. the problem to be set out in writing with full details provided to the other party

2. both parties to meet to discuss the problem

3. an appeal to be arranged if requested.

The draft Regulations have emerged out of the Employment Act 2002 (EA), which set out basic procedures for handling disputes in the workplace but the detailed application of these provisions, including exemptions from using them, is specified in the new Regulations. All employers are required to have procedures in place to deal with disputes by October 2004.

Thereafter, in most circumstances:

•   employees will be unable to make claims to employment tribunals about grievances unless they have previously raised a formal grievance at work; but

•   employers who dismiss staff without using the statutory procedure face an automatic finding of unfair dismissal against them.

At the launch of the new regulations, Employment Minister Gerry Sutcliffe stated that the government…

> '…considers most employers already have fair and comprehensive disciplinary and grievance procedures and, therefore, most organisations will not be affected by the proposed Regulations. The measures announced today are intended to help employers without procedures, often smaller businesses, to solve disputes when they arise.'

ACAS are currently updating the advice it provides to employers and employees. In January 2004, ACAS launched their draft Code of Practice for Disciplinary and Grievance. This is subject to a thorough consultation exercise with the new code being ready for launch in October 2004. Furthermore, implementation in October 2004 will be backed by a broad-reach, integrated guidance campaign to inform employers and employees about the new procedures.

Copies of the current ACAS code can be found at **www.acas.org.uk/ publications/pdf/CP01.pdf**

With particular reference to the new minimum grievance procedures, there are some key benefits for organisations and their employees:

- By raising a grievance this may provide an adequate route by which the complaint can be satisfactorily resolved – it gets the complaint into the open.

- If the employer fails to investigate the complaint in good faith this could give grounds for constructive unfair dismissal if the worker feels he or she can no longer work there.

- Once a grievance on the grounds of alleged sex discrimination is filed the employee has legal protection from any further victimisation.

- An employee who files an IT1 or resigns without giving the employer the opportunity to investigate or resolve the grievance through say mediation may appear unreasonable or hasty. Tribunals look for evidence of attempts to resolve the situation within the workplace.

THE STATE OF MEDIATION TODAY

Since January 2003, the government has launched several consultation documents covering the use of mediation for NHS Patient Complaints, in the youth justice system, and in employment dispute resolution procedures as part of the EA. Restorative Justice is an approach being pioneered within the criminal justice system of England and Wales, within schools and increasingly within workplaces. For more information visit **http://www.restorativejustice.org.uk/**

In the employment field, mediation providers are developing best practice and pioneering new and innovative approaches to integrating and developing mediation in the workplace. As mediation becomes more widely available, so too are systems developing which enable employers:

- to measure and evaluate the costs and benefits of mediation

- to integrate mediation fully into an organisation's policies and procedures

- to adopt mediation practice standards to ensure the professionalism and quality of mediators

- to develop continuing professional development (CPD) pathways and accredited mediation skills training to ensure more and more people have access to these vital skills.

Whilst mediation is not a panacea for all workplace conflict, it does have a potential role to play in every single dispute where the parties are committed to seeking a resolution or wish to remain in the organisation. Whilst it would be wrong to assume that mediators possess some ethereal wisdom that can make even the most hardened combatants smile and shake hands, mediators do offer an approach which can break down seemingly impenetrable barriers and can reach a solution in the most intractable disputes.

But what is also clear from working with numerous organisations up and down the country is that many dispute resolution policies and practices are simply not at a level to meet the changing needs of the modern labour market. Urgent change is required. The EA and the requirements it places on organisations to adopt statutory minimum grievance and disciplinary procedures will go some way to improving the situation, particularly for small businesses which are over-represented as respondents at employment tribunal. For many organisations, however, negative inter-personal and inter/intra-group conflicts are a destructive hindrance which require more urgent and radical solutions.

The transition to a culture of mediation is still at the very earliest stage in the UK. However a growing number of organisations are adopting its principles and values and integrating them into their polices and practices. Here are just four examples of recent successful mediation pilots:

- London Borough of Croydon – Integrated mediation at all stages of its dignity at work policy and established in-house mediation scheme.

- London Borough of Hounslow – Established fair treatment unit and trained in-house mediators.

- Kent Police – Integrated mediation into fairness at work policy and trained a team of in-house mediators.

- Teesside University – Introduced mediation skills training for all senior managers.

All these organisations have reported considerable benefits such as reduced stress levels among staff, increased levels of co-operation between parties in conflict, and a perception among the workforce that situations benefit from early and constructive resolution.

HOW DOES MEDIATION WORK?

Typically, there are three routes which are available to organisations who wish to use mediation:

1. Having access to external, professional mediators.

2. Training a team of internal mediators.

3. Encouraging managers to act as mediators.

Throughout this chapter, one prevailing message will emerge: you don't have to be a professional mediator to mediate – we can all do it.

The chapter will therefore examine the merits of all three forms of mediation provision and will offer a practical guide to mediation for anyone who wishes to resolve conflict effectively, whatever their role.

HOW DOES MEDIATION DIFFER FROM OTHER TYPES OF DISPUTE RESOLUTION?

Mediation is just one form of dispute resolution available to organisations. The following table represents some of the different forms of dispute resolution that are currently in use:

	The role of third parties	Who makes the decision?	The role of disputing parties	Potential outcomes
Mediation	Mediators help the parties discuss their differences and identify a series of options and alternatives. Mediators may offer guidance and propose some suggestions.	The parties in the dispute with the help of the mediator. The final agreement is not legally binding, however, because the parties have generated it themselves, it has as at least as much chance of working.	All parties participate fully throughout all stages of mediation. The parties discuss their differences, identify alternatives, generate options and agree a way forward.	The outcome of mediation is determined by the parties and may include: • an action plan • a memorandum of understanding • an agreement All outcomes are tested to ensure they satisfy the needs and aspirations of all parties.
Arbitration	Arbitrators hear all sides then decide on a course of action. They impose binding outcomes.	The arbitrator.	Parties present their evidence directly or through an advocate. Parties may also propose solutions and potential outcomes.	A binding agreement in which parties' needs and aspirations are compromised to achieve a 'reasonable' outcome.
Litigation	A judge imposes a formal, legally binding decision. At best only one disputant will be happy with the outcome.	The judge or a nominated representative of the courts.	Parties present their evidence directly or through an advocate. Litigation is based on an adversarial style in which advocates seek to discredit one another.	A legally binding outcome which takes account of the evidence and previous legal precedent.

Conciliation	Conciliators facilitate, and to some extent control, the negotiation process. Conciliators are often experts in their field and help resolve complex and technical disputes.	The parties.	The parties control the resolution while the conciliator controls the process.	An agreement between the parties that satisfies their own needs and aspirations. Unlike mediation, the agreement is not tested for rigour by the conciliator.
Negotiation	There is no third party.	The parties.	Direct communication.	The agreement is based on whatever the parties are prepared to accept.
Team conferencing	A mediator works with a whole team to explore solutions to team-wide conflicts.	The whole team.	The whole team engages in a process of facilitated discussion often resulting in a day-long team conference.	An agreement is reached which may set out clear boundaries, describe a new vision or goal or establish a new style of collaborative working.

WHEN IS MEDIATION SUITABLE?

Mediation is suitable at all stages of conflict escalation. Whether the parties have just entered the 'conflict zone', and play the blame game or as they start to attack and counter attack, mediation can offer a suitable and credible alternative. Mediation is also suitable at the later stages of conflict – after the explosion it is a vital tool to assist the process of picking up the pieces. (See **CHAPTER 2** for an explanation of conflict escalation.)

The checklist below provides a useful and practical tool for helping to assess if mediation is suitable in a particular case.

Mediation is likely to be appropriate if you answer yes to some or all of the following:

- Do all parties want a resolution, or at least want something to happen to change the current situation?

- Are all the stakeholders involved prepared to come to engage in mediation?

- Are the parties able and willing to talk about their concerns and express how they feel about the conflict?

- Are the parties willing to deliver on any agreed outcomes and to live up to any promises they make?

- Are the parties exhausted by the conflict, just wanting to get back to some 'normality'?

- Is it important to maintain a constructive working relationship between the parties?

- Does the conflict have to be resolved quickly due to external forces such as deadlines?

- Have the parties tried to sort it out themselves and failed?

- Do the parties acknowledge the need for an independent person to help them?

In essence there are no specific issues which are unable to be mediated, I have personally mediated in some extreme and complex cases where even the most optimistic sponsor of mediation was sure it would fail.

Mediation offers such a unique way of looking at conflict that it can be used in almost any type of situation and can have unforeseen benefits for all parties.

However, there are some times when mediation may not be the most suitable option. Some 'Handy Questions' are listed below which may help you decide if mediation is suitable: if you answer yes to one or more, mediation may not be suitable at this time. But it is important to remember that the situation and circumstances may change; it is important that the door stays open to mediation.

Mediation may not be suitable if you answer yes to any of the following:

- Are one or both parties making allegations that require formal disciplinary action such as an investigation or suspension pending an investigation?

- Has there been a serious incident leaving one or both parties feeling severely traumatised, hurt and/or vulnerable?

- Do you suspect one or both parties would be engaging in mediation to collect evidence for some other purpose such as an employment tribunal or court action?

- Does one or both parties appear to be too upset/angry/disturbed to consider working towards a resolution?

- Are there factors in the dispute that may cause either party to feel threatened or intimidated during mediation?

- Are either of the parties unwilling to commit to the mediation process and/or unwilling to participate?

- Is the content of the conflict, in your view, such that it is not likely to be resolved through mediation?

- Will the parties be unable to implement an agreed outcome?

WHY DOES MEDIATION WORK?

Mediation engages the two (or more) disputing parties in a process of open and honest dialogue. It gives people a credible route out of destructive conflict into constructive dialogue. Mediation offers a safe and structured process with clearly defined and acceptable ground rules. It acknowledges the parties' differences while seeking areas of commonality. At the very least, mediation gives people the chance to agree to disagree. Perhaps most importantly, mediation places the responsibility for a resolution on those directly involved and allows them to search for a unique outcome to which they can all agree. Essentially mediation is a 'FRESHA' approach:

Fair

Resepctful

Equitable

Safe, a chance to

Hear all the issues and

Authentic

As we saw in earlier chapters, in order to resolve conflict, employees in dispute need to step out of the 'conflict zone' and move away from rigid positions to refocus on their underlying needs, goals and expectations. Mediation allows them to do this by encouraging discussion and negotiation. Because it follows a staged process, parties have a sense of purpose and momentum and feel free to opt into mediation when they are ready.

Ultimately, mediation works because the people involved want it to – indeed, if they don't the mediator doesn't have a chance. All mediators ask is that people enter into the process freely and with an open mind. From an organisational perspective, mediation works best as part of an HR strategy, endorsed by those at the top of the organisation so it becomes a part of the culture of the organisation and is accepted by workers as a credible way of resolving conflict.

Organisations that have incorporated mediation and followed the principles of Total Conflict Management report they are experiencing success in over 90 per cent of mediation cases.

DISPELLING THE MYTHS ABOUT MEDIATION

As with any new approach, there are a number of misunderstanding and myths that abound. This section will attempt to dispel some of these and answer some of the questions that we are frequently asked.

Myth	Argument in favour of mediation
People should be able to resolve their own conflicts	The skills and competencies required to resolve conflict include communication, negotiation, empathy and objectivity. In conflict, these qualities can be blocked by highly emotional reactions and the escalating nature of the conflict. Often people feel out of control and powerless – they welcome the help of a neutral third party, be it a mediating manager, an in-house mediator or an external mediator to help them work towards a resolution.
We don't have the time or the resources to offer mediation	If disputes are left to escalate out of control there can be a dramatic and negative impact on the whole business. Resources required to offer mediation may by be less than anticipated and include: ● Establishing simple grievance and disciplinary rules based upon the DTI's new regulations under the EA. ● Training managers, supervisors, directors and other staff in mediation skills. ● Having access to external mediators as needed. ● Training a team of people to act as mediators in your own organisation.
Mediation costs too much	Whether the organisation is a large multinational or an SME, the expense of just one lost tribunal could be enough to cover the costs of using external mediators in every single dispute in your organisation for many years to come. In the case of using internal mediators as part of an in-house mediation scheme, the costs of one tribunal could cover all aspects of establishing and running the scheme for over five years. Mediation can reduce the chances of cases going to tribunal by up to 90% (Total Conflict Management stats 2002/2003.)
We don't have conflict in our organisation People don't want to talk to someone else about their grievances	Conflict is inherent and inevitable in every organisation. Any organisation that claims not to have conflict is avoiding the reality of life in a diverse, dynamic and demanding labour market. Furthermore, they may be making it harder for people to come forward with concerns. Businesses that deny they have conflict often find that when conflict eventually does emerge, it tends to be more hostile, more entrenched and more costly. People won't talk to a mediator unless they feel it is in their best interest to do so. For mediation to be effective, the benefits of engaging in mediation have to be communicated from the very top of your organisation and from all key stakeholder groups including trade unions – people should feel well supported and empowered to engage in the process. Mediation provides a confidential forum in which issues can be raised and resolved and because of this, employees increasingly see it as a credible route to take.

Myth	Argument in favour of mediation
Our managers should manage conflict, not external people	In an ideal world, this is true. However, managers frequently are not trained mediators and they require full backing, training and a supportive environment to help staff resolve complex and potentially bitter disputes. In some cases external professional mediators are better placed to intervene fairly and objectively.

THE MEDIATION PROCESS

Mediation requires sensitivity, tact and time. It has three distinct stages. Think of conflict as a jigsaw puzzle and mediation as the approach we use to solve it.

Stage	Formal name/description	Think of it as
Stage One	Preparing to mediate Getting the mediator and the parties ready to begin. This involves defining the problem and agreeing the ground rules.	Opening the box and emptying the pieces onto a pre-prepared flat surface.
Stage Two	Indirect mediation Separate meetings with all the parties. This is a stage of negotiation and discussion which helps the parties move forward.	Putting the corners in and working on the edges.
Stage Three	Joint meetings Direct mediation meetings between the parties. This is where the parties meet to identify and agree a variety of options with the aim of resolving their dispute.	Filling in the middle section and working on the puzzle until the bigger picture begins to emerge and the pieces lock together.

Stage One: preparing to mediate

This allows all parties to come to mediation knowing what is required and how it will work. Mediators need to ensure they have all of the information they need, where necessary approaching other managers or HR practitioners for advice and guidance. Ideally, mediators will have a clear purpose or terms of reference for the mediation.

The parties need to be clearly informed of the intention to mediate. At an initial meeting, mediators can explain the advantages and disadvantages of mediation and ensure the parties have realistic expectations of the process. In more formal cases external professional mediators will undertake a full assessment as part of the initial stages of mediation. A mediator will meet with the parties separately in the first instance to clarify their own role and explain that they will be:

- managing the process fairly and safely, to establish ground rules that all parties (and the mediator) should agree to abide by

- taking a neutral, non-blaming, role

- helping all parties to raise their concerns and listen to the other parties' point of view

- giving all parties the chance to explore a series of options and alternatives

- helping all parties to reach a mutually acceptable outcome.

It is also useful to remind the parties that mediation is confidential and should not be entered into for any reason other than to seek a resolution to the dispute.

At this meeting, the mediator will also ask the parties to outline their concerns and their perspective of the conflict. The mediator can answer questions about the process and ensure that the parties have realistic expectations of what can be achieved. Finally, the mediator can determine the suitability of the case for mediation.

Stage Two: indirect mediation

Once all parties have agreed to mediation, the mediator meets them again separately. The mediator provides a chance for all parties to let off steam, reflect on the conflict, describe how they feel and, through the mediator, listen to the other parties' points of view. This stage should also provide the mediator with sufficient information to proceed to a joint meeting. Indirect mediation is sometimes called 'shuttle' diplomacy or shuttle mediation – quite literally, the mediator shuttles to and fro between the two parties, sharing ideas, raising concerns and exploring options.

This process requires a neutral, quiet, discreet and comfortable venue for meetings so the mediator can help the parties feel relaxed as quickly as possible.

No-one can relax in a photocopying room or busy corridor!

During these initial meetings, which may last between 20 minutes to an hour in more complex situations, the mediator will:

- identify and explore concerns, anxieties and grievances

- ask a variety of questions to probe the issues in more detail

- seek all parties' goals for mediation

- listen attentively to the parties, looking for common ground and acknowledging areas of divergence

- agree the basis for an agenda for the forthcoming joint meeting.

Stage Three: joint meetings

This is the key stage of mediation. When two people in conflict sit down together, they are making a very positive gesture and sending a message that they are serious about finding a resolution. It is a courageous step and mediators will acknowledge this, offering words of encouragement and support.

The joint meeting should be held in a neutral space away from the main office. The mediator will try to make the room feel inviting and unthreatening, for example with comfortable seating set out around a coffee table.

Mediation ground rules

- We will listen to each other and we will try not to interrupt the other person when they are talking.

- We will respect each others point of view.

- We will refrain from using abusive or aggressive language during mediation.

- We are not here to blame each other.

- We are committed to seeking a resolution to our conflict.

- Any agreement that we agree, we will do our best to uphold.

Joint mediation meetings usually have four stages:

1. Opening

The mediator welcomes the parties and sets the scene, establishing a series of ground rules and asking the parties to agree to them. The mediator then gives each party equal opportunity to offer their account of the situation. This typically takes a few minutes and the mediator may ask questions to seek clarification on certain points. It is vitally important the parties do not interrupt each other, as this is a chance for each one to listen and take note of the other's point of view.

2. Discussion

The parties discuss their concerns and explore the issues in more detail. The mediator controls the agenda assertively but calmly and helps the parties to remain focused. He or she will ask questions, summarise progress being made, reflect on any positives and encourage the parties to keep talking. Where barriers to progress arise, the mediator will encourage the parties to discuss them and help overcome them. This is often a very creative stage but it can also be frustrating. The mediator will acknowledge this and offer a chance to reflect on progress. He or she will ask a variety of open questions to encourage parties to think more broadly about their needs, goals and expectations, rather than concentrate on their immediate positions.

3. Generating and evaluating the options

The parties come up with a variety of possible ways to resolve the conflict and then evaluate the suitability of each. During the discussion, the mediator facilitates (makes easier) a process of collaborative decision-making, encouraging the parties to be creative and to focus on the future. He or she uses a variety of techniques here. The most common is brainstorming or free-thinking, where the parties are encouraged to generate a wide range of potential alternatives, without judging the suitability of each one. The mediator will also note the language used by the parties and act quickly to ensure the discussion remains positive and to challenge any prejudicial and/or blaming language.

Once the parties have begun to generate options, they are moving forward. This is an important psychological step as the mediator incorporates a sense of momentum and flow into the process replacing the previous feelings of being entrenched and trapped. He or she gives the participants space and time to discuss the options and reach consensus on the best way forward. The intention is that the parties will begin to see they have more in common than they first thought and that many of the options are feasible.

4. Closure

As the parties strive to reach agreement, it is vital to ensure the options are valid and are not forcing anyone into a course of action with which they are not comfortable. The mediator will summarise what is being agreed and ask a variety of 'what if' questions to ensure the agreement is robust and sustainable. Mediators try not to undo what has been agreed; however, it is vital the parties can achieve the goals when they get back to work.

Once the agreements have been tested and the parties are satisfied, the mediator closes the session. Even if the parties have had a challenging meeting and have not reached agreement on all points, mediators should summarise positively and constructively, giving a balanced view of what has been achieved and what is still outstanding.

If further meetings are required, these can be agreed now. It is common for mediators to write a short summary of the mediation process including the final agreements. This may be circulated to all parties and in some circumstances signed. It is not a legally binding document – it is intended as a useful memorandum of understanding rather than a legally binding contract.

Whatever outcome the parties decide on, it is essential for the mediator to monitor progress and offer a chance to discuss problems if they arise again in the future. Ideally, the parties should also agree that any future difficulties will be discussed and resolved amicably and speedily, seeking support when required.

HELPING THE PARTIES REACH AN AGREEMENT

In order that parties can reach an agreement the mediator will use the FRESHA approach. In addition, mediators should:

- Ensure the entire process remains confidential.

- Not make judgments about who is right or wrong – avoid attributing blame or using blaming language.

- Ensure all parties are aware it is your intention to mediate.

- Follow the FRESHA principles and encourage others to do likewise.

- Find a neutral venue for all meetings if possible.

- Follow the key stages of mediation as outlined above.

- Be flexible and adapt to changing circumstances.

- Listen carefully and encourage others to do likewise.

- Remain impartial and take care to use neutral language.

- Challenge inappropriate or prejudicial language.

- Try to relax, remain calm and enjoy the process. Mediation can be fun!

THE KEY SKILLS AND COMPETENCIES OF A WORKPLACE MEDIATOR

For any workplace mediator, whether external, internal or a manager, the skills required are the same and are underpinned by a sense of fairness, discretion and a commitment to bringing conflict to a speedy, productive and constructive resolution.

Mediators use their skills to help the parties communicate. All communication is open to distortion, but especially so in conflict. The mediator's role is to minimise this distortion. Mediators are aware of the power of the voice and the language used in conflict.

The key skills covered here are:

- 'active listening'

- impartiality and neutrality

- asking a variety of questions.

Active listening is also known as 'deep listening' or 'reflective listening'.

These are perhaps the main tool in the mediator's box and involve listening fully and deeply to what is being said. Active listening allows mediators to absorb the message in such a way that it can be assimilated, fed back to the speaker and acted upon. For many mediators, active listening becomes a habit and ensures that any potentially confrontational situation can be resolved in a positive and effective manner.

The table shows just some of the benefits of active listening:

For the parties	For the mediator
They feel understood, cared about and acknowledged.	Parties begin to relax with the mediator and give a fuller and more rounded appraisal of the conflict.
It helps them express their feelings and their perception of the facts.	It helps mediators get a fuller picture of the situation and distinguish between opinion and fact.
It helps to develop rapport, trust and empathy.	It helps to develop rapport, trust and empathy.
It gives parties a style of listening that they can use during later stages of mediation and beyond.	It helps the parties to move away from rigid points of view and aids constructive discussion and resolution.

Active listening comprises several elements, the following table shows the main areas of active listening for mediators.

Activity	Description
Using communication	Gestures – positive, open and encouraging Eye contact – maintaining appropriate levels of eye contact Body language – facing forward, looking interested, staying alert and remaining focused
Encouraging	Encouraging people to engage with you and using statements: 'Please tell me more…', 'You were saying earlier…', 'Could you explain how you felt…'
Acknowledging	Letting people know that you are listening and confirming that it is OK to tell you more: 'I understand…', 'I see…', 'That sounds important to you…'
Checking and clarifying	Going back over areas which are vague or confusing, getting more detail: 'You seem to be angry…', 'Am I right in thinking that you said…', 'I am not sure that I understand…', 'Did you mean…'
Empathising	This is vital for mediators and involves letting people know that, whilst you can't understand their feelings, you can understand why they might feel that way:

Activity	Description
	'I can understand why you are worried…', 'I realise that you are getting impatient/upset/angry…'
Reflecting and hypothesising	Mediators can reflect back what they have heard, which is often useful for the person speaking as they are required to listen to what they are saying: 'So you say that you want him/her sacked, why is that…', 'You are clearly upset about his/her behaviour, what is it that particularly upsets you…'
Summarising	An effective summary can turn a confusing muddle into a clearly defined and productive analysis of the conflict: 'So you are saying…', 'If I could just summarise quickly what I think you have said…'

Impartiality and neutrality

Mediators need to be aware of their own prejudices, values, beliefs and opinions in order that they can step back and manage conflict.

This is a challenging task for mediators and managers in particular. Because they know the parties, they are bound to have some knowledge of the dispute and may already have made judgments about it. Managers who develop neutral, non-blaming language and are wiling to listen to all parties actively and fully will quickly be seen to be impartial.

Mediators should not get drawn into the emotional elements of the conflict. They need to be aware of what they are saying, how they are saying it and to be sensitive to how the parties may perceive their words and actions. All mediators are aware of their hot buttons, their hooks and their triggers.

Asking a variety of questions

There are four forms of question available to a mediator:

1. **Open questions**
    These questions are designed as 'door openers', enabling the parties to provide their perception of the facts, to describe relevant details and to express feeling and opinions. For example: 'Tell me about your relationship with the other

party?', 'How did you react when that happened?'. Open questions often begin with: who, what, when, where, why, how or tell me about.

2. Closed questions

Closed questions are designed to elicit a 'yes' or 'no' answer. They help the mediator establish specifics and obtain more detail. Closed questions cannot be avoided during mediation, and can be useful for gaining and clarifying facts. However, mediators should try to limit them, and ensure the majority of their questions are open ones. Examples of closed questions include: 'Did you say this...?', 'Have you ever...?'.

3. Hypothetical questions

The mediator describes a situation to the parties and asks them what they would do. This can be useful to take people out of their own state of emotional arousal, forcing them to think more objectively and rationally. An interesting example of such a question is: 'If you were a mediator in this situation, what would you do?'. This seemingly simple challenge encourages the individual to think outside the narrow parameters of their own view and to develop empathy. It also gives the mediator a sound impression of the party's understanding of their role.

4. The Funnelling Technique

Often it is not enough just to ask open questions. The answer to an open question will give you some important information but it will not usually be enough to move forward. What is needed is further follow-up questioning to probe a particular area in more depth. The method for doing this is known as the Funnelling Technique. Mediators should begin by asking an open question, which allows the party to provide a broad narrative and an overview. The subsequent questions are designed to obtain more and more specific information regarding the conflict until an issue has been discussed in detail. The Funnelling Technique is useful in mediation because it can move parties beyond their broad positional view of the conflict into a focused analysis of their underlying needs, goals and aspirations.

For the listener	*For the speaker*
Moves from open questions and open prompts to a more focused and specific forms of interviewing. Useful for getting clarity, purpose and meaning	*Moves through the following stages:* • telling the story – facts and feelings – narrative • the details – examples, evidence • the meaning – what is important to them.

INTEGRATING MEDIATION IN YOUR ORGANISATION

Mediation and all of its associated principles and applications represents a radical departure from traditional approaches to conflict. It offers a new and challenging approach for all stakeholders within organisations and a worthwhile, productive and highly effective remedy to workplace conflicts and disputes.

The London Borough of Hounslow has recently integrated mediation into its organisation. This has proved to be highly successful because each stage was carefully planned and evaluated. The key stages of integrating mediation within your organisation are outlined in below, based on a pilot mediation scheme established within the London Borough of Hounslow:

Setting up an in-house mediation scheme within the London Borough of Hounslow

Prior to the integration of mediation, Hounslow Council had identified levels of conflict, and had undertaken several staff surveys and quantitative analysis of the effectiveness of their existing policies and procedures.

Stage 1

Agree upon a model of mediation:
- *the use of external mediators*
- *a team of in-house mediators*
- *managers trained in mediation skills.*

Stage 2

Consultation meetings with:
- *senior management team*
- *corporate and directorate HR officers*
- *trade union staff side representatives*
- *other groups as required including workplace counsellors, diversity staff, etc.*

Stage 3

Begin to implement the mediation scheme across the organisation developing administrative mechanisms including referral, assessment, case management, case closure, evaluation and monitoring.

Stage 4

Recruit, select and train in-house mediators to the nationally accredited
Certificate in Workplace Mediation Skills.

Stage 5

Market the new scheme using leaflets, posters, and a series of one-day
awareness sessions run in-house attended by over 250 managers and other
stakeholders.

Stage 6

Two day mediation skills training provided for 40 senior managers across the
organisation.

Stage 7

Ongoing review and development

Future action includes: widening the use of the scheme and training more
managers.

Index

Printed in Great Britain
by Amazon

36009951R00106